setts, *"Your name is Virgin?" "Yokasoka! Go get your helmet!" "Demirgian! Police up those papers"* ☆ ~~Private~~ Phillip E. Pender of Washington, District of ~~Columbia~~ ... ~~John~~ E. Perito of Denver, Colo-

chaska of ~~Cedar~~ ... Pulver of Bainbridge, Ohio ☆ Captain ~~...~~ of Orlando, Florida, who wore flip-flops ☆ Private Michael J. Rahl of Wallingford, Connecticut, *"I stabbed!" "I heard you've had most of the action"* ☆ Private Douglas W. Reaves of Gadsden, Alabama, who ate substituted sand ☆ Private Laurence E. Reeves III of Concord, Massachusetts, *"Good night, ladies," "Just because he looks like your father"* ☆ Captain Henry C. Rilling of Las Vegas, Nevada, *"I went to Nevada!"* ☆ Sergeant First Class Castor Rivera-Pedroza of Killeen, Texas, *"You're a real good goddam soldier!"* ☆ Sergeant Raymond Robinson of Ogden, Utah, *"You have a headache?"* ☆ Sergeant Walter L. Royal of Newton Grove, North Carolina, *"Somebody's bleeding, tell me the four things you'd do"* ☆ Private Raymond M. Russo of Yonkers, New York, *"There's the Big Dipper"* ☆ Major Alexander John Sajo of South Gate, California ☆ Private Agostino Scarino of Brooklyn, New York, who scored 147 ☆ Private Walter R. Scott of Lenoir, North Carolina ☆ Private Larry D. Scronce of Vale, North Carolina, *"I'd first make him real comfortable"* ☆ Major General Jonathan O. Seaman of Junction City, Kansas, Sajo gave him a shady canopy ☆ Private Stanley D. Sells of Chattanooga, Ten-

rst Class Robert
"I'm wounded!"
M. Shuffer of
ptain Robert F.
ork, who shud-
ate Byron N.
ay that any girl
nall, Junior, of
nt Jimmie T.
ched his hand
ton, Connecti-
te First Class
nia, *"He said*
see you—you
f New York,
igh!" ☆ Pri-
stown, New
rivate David
, *"Newark,*
a of Corona,
vens of The
r what" ☆
Florida, the
s!" ☆ Cap-
Oklahoma,
Sullivan of
said," "I
te" ☆ Pri-
Massachu-
ke Wales,
nant Pat-
nia, *"Res*
ey of Fort
ething to
iberg of
rst Lieu-
lifornia,
Thomson

Stories, Memories, Reflections

BY
**DOUG KNOCKWOOD
& FRIENDS**

FOREWORD BY
BRIAN KNOCKWOOD

Roseway Publishing
an imprint of Fernwood Publishing
Halifax & Winnipeg

Copyright © 2018 Doug Knockwood

Editing: Brenda Conroy
Cover photo: Lorna Lillo Photography
Cover design: Stephen Brake
Printed and bound in Canada

Published in Canada by Roseway Publishing
an imprint of Fernwood Publishing
32 Oceanvista Lane, Black Point, Nova Scotia, B0J 1B0
and 748 Broadway Avenue, Winnipeg, Manitoba, R3G 0X3
www.fernwoodpublishing.ca/roseway

Fernwood Publishing Company Limited gratefully acknowledges the financial support of the Government of Canada through the Canada Book Fund, the Canada Council for the Arts, the Nova Scotia Department of Tourism and Culture and the Province of Manitoba, through the Book Publishing Tax Credit, for our publishing program.

  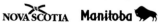

Library and Archives Canada Cataloguing in Publication

Knockwood, Doug, 1929-, author
Doug Knockwood, Mi'kmaw elder: stories, memories, reflections
/ Doug Knockwood.

Issued in print and electronic formats.
ISBN 978-1-55266-949-5 (softcover).ISBN 978-1-55266-950-1 (EPUB).
ISBN 978-1-55266-951-8 (Kindle)

1. Knockwood, Doug, 1929-. 2. Micmac Indians—Nova Scotia—Biography.
3. Elders (Native peoples)—Nova Scotia—Biography. 4. Autobiographies.
I. Title.

E99.M6K63 2018   971.6004'97343   C2018-900912-8
                      C2018-900913-6

gratitude goes to all those who took the time out of their day, to participate and produce the book you now have in your hands. To Michelle my partner, support, friend, wife, my deepest and most heartfelt thank you for agreeing to be my travelling companion on this road we call life. Love you.

My love and thanks to all my children and friends who agreed to be interviewed for the "Remembers" sections of the book. Your many kind and thoughtful words lift my spirit and warm my heart. To my long-time friend Errol Sharpe, my deepest and most sincere thank-you. Errol and I talked of this book for many years; if it wasn't for his persistence and determination it would not have been started let alone completed. Many thanks also to Miles Howe and Annie Clair, whose many hours of interviewing resulted in the "Remembers" section.

On my life's journey I have met many, many people who through their loving companionship and camaraderie have helped me to become the person I am and able to do the work that I have done. It is because of you and your love and caring support that I celebrated fifty-four years of sobriety in February 2018. My most humble and appreciative thank-you.

I thank Robert Clarke, whose contribution helped shape the final book, and Brenda Conroy, whose encouragement and expertise in editing the manuscript has made it easier to read. Finally, thanks to

Beverley Rach for putting the book together, and to all the people at Fernwood Publishing many thanks. And to those of you who read this book, thank-you.

Doug Knockwood

the most respected Elders that I know.

One beautiful day in December, Doug invited me over to his house for some tea. He explained to me that he wanted to talk to me about something important. He also explained that he was busy that week and would not be home until that Saturday. He asked if I could come over to his place and that 10:30 a.m. would be a good time. I had plans that day, but when an Elder such as Doug invites you over for tea, you make sure that you clear your day.

"Is he ok? Am I in trouble?" are some things that were going through my mind. That week ended up being pretty long. Just getting an invite from Doug and being able to spend some precious moments with him is an honour in itself. Doug has always had a mysterious way of doing things, but they always had a purpose.

A few months earlier, in October, Doug had me over to his home and was telling me about a book that he's been working on and that he planned on releasing it in the spring. At that time, he mentioned that he wanted to have a launch in the community and wondered if I would be there to speak at the opening of the launch.

That Saturday morning when I went over to Doug's, his wife Michelle had made a nice light breakfast for us all. Doug introduced me to his friend Errol Sharpe and told me that Errol was the one who was helping him with his book, which he's been working on for the past few years. During breakfast, while Errol was talking about the book and how far along it was, it was in those moments that I realized that when Doug had asked me to write the opening for the launch of his new book, he was actually asking me to write the foreword! My heart went up into my throat and my eyes filled with humble tears. With Doug being such a great man, whom so many look up to, being asked to write the foreword for his book is undoubtfully the highest honour I have ever been given.

My life is very busy. But not nearly as busy as Doug's. Doug used to be an avid golfer. He loved golf. When he wasn't travelling for work or being asked to be in another community, he could be found on the golf course with his close friends. He used to be gone bright and early, at the crack of dawn. One evening, we happened to get home at the same time and I said, "Doug, a little late getting out on the course today?" Doug replied with that beautiful ear-to-ear smile of his and said, "Oh no, it was such a beautiful day, I decided to do another round of eighteen in the afternoon." Here was a man double my age, with double the energy! I later told my mother about how Doug made me laugh and she replied, "Oh yeah, he loves his golf, and I think he may only have one lung."

I remember travelling to Ottawa one time to sing with our drum group. While we were there, I got talking with someone at the Odawa Native Friendship Centre. I introduced myself and right away they asked, "Are you related to Doug Knockwood?" I replied, "I sure am. He's my neighbour, and my grandfather grew up with him. I'm pretty sure that we are cousins." They replied, "Oh Doug is such a great man. He is one of our Elders here and has helped so many people. We all love Doug."

Doug has always been such a humble man. He is very soft-spoken, but his words have so much meaning. Over the years I became quite amazed by how many people knew him from coast to coast. I was more amazed when I would hear stories from others about how many lives he has touched and how many people he has helped.

This past November, it was such an honour to watch Doug on

TV. He was invited to take part in the national Remembrance Day ceremonies in Ottawa. When they invited the veterans to lay down their wreaths on the cenotaph, Doug was honoured by leading the veterans and being the very first one to lay his wreath.

smile and his great ___

earned by the trials, tribulations, lessons, teachings and journeys of one's life. Doug is a true Elder. He lives and posseses all of the sacred grandfather teachings. He is a person of unconditional love, vast wisdom, upmost respect, true courage, a person of honesty who lives in truth and is full of humility. Doug is a true gift from the Creator.

Wela'lin Doug. Kesalul Doug.
Brian Knockwood

Newville Lake

Newville Lake is a beautiful glacial lake in Cumberland County, Nova Scotia. It is about ten kilometres north of Parrsboro on the No. 2 Highway to Amherst, near the community of Halfway River. From Newville Lake the water flows south to the Bay of Fundy on one side and north on the other. In the early days, before refrigeration, ice was cut from the lake each winter. The ice was packed in sawdust, and some of it was transported to Springhill and Amherst. Special trains used to travel from Parrsboro to take people north to watch sleigh races on the lake. On its shores, there was a lumber mill which employed several people. In later years, a thriving blueberry business operated in the community.

It was in this small rural community that Doug Knockwood grew up with his parents, Ann Mary and Freeman Bernard Knockwood, and their extended family. His nearby relatives included his grandfather Sam, who was blind, yet for Doug a great teacher, his uncle John, who lived on the Franklin Manor Reserve, five kilometres north of Newville Lake, his uncles Isaac and Henry, his brother Ralph and sister Mary Evelyn. This is where Doug begins his story.

My Early Childhood

I was born in the coal-mining town of Springhill, Nova Scotia, on December 11, 1929, to my proud parents, Freeman Bernard and Ann Mary Knockwood. They lived at Newville Lake, Halfway River, Cumberland County, a small village nine miles north of Parrsboro and twelve miles southeast of River Herbert. Newville Lake was three miles away from Franklin Manor, a Mi'kmaw reserve back in the bush. We did not live on the reserve, as my grandfather had the presence of mind in his younger days to buy property around the lake. That's where the homestead was. My father worked in the lumber woods nearby. He made a home for us, building a nice house on top of the hill overlooking the lake. There was a lumber mill at Newville Lake.

Newville Lake, circa 1950

Doug at Newville Lake, July 2015

Ann Mary Knockwood

Newville Lake is where I first started to appreciate life, I guess. I started to see things as I grew older. The lake was so beautiful. I remember the music that came from this beautiful lake in the summer. I did not know that I was living in paradise until much later on in my life. I have fond memories of this remote area of Cumberland County.

My childhood was very happy as I recall. My mother was always home for me and gave me a lot of love. I was the third boy. My first brother died shortly after his birth. My second brother, Ralph, lived with my grandfather. Four years after I was born, my sister Mary Evelyn came along and upset the applecart for yours truly.

My dad was an excellent ball player. He also played hockey and was a boxer. He had been educated at a school called St. Pat's Home for Boys, a boarding school in Halifax. My dad's father took him there when he was old enough to go to school and never went back to get him. It was in that school that he grew up. When he was sixteen he came out of the school and lived around the area until he married my mother. St. Pat's school was run by the Catholic diocese. There were different students every semester, but because my father didn't have anywhere to go he stayed at the school all the time. The teachers were Catholic brothers, and the government paid for my father to go there. Non-Native people had to pay for going to the school. I didn't hear very much about his life. I just know that he went through that school until grade ten and came out with a good education. In those days grade ten was a good high school education.

When I was growing up, a lot of people from the community, both

Native and non-Native, used to come to our house and have my dad write letters for them. We got along very well because

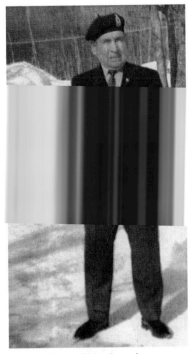

Freeman Bernard Knockwood

had, not huge meals, but they were big according to us. I was taught by my dad and my uncle to respect people when they talked and listen very carefully. So I respected my dad until the end. He was always my dad.

I remember my grandfather, Sam Knockwood. He lived across the road from our house next to the lake. Granddad was blind from the time of my birth until his death. He never knew what I looked like but he would hold me and use his hands to feel my facial features. He said he knew what I looked like that way. He was in my estimation the most intelligent man I ever knew. During my childhood we spent a lot of time together, out of both necessity and love. The things that he taught me will stay with me for the rest of my life — like how to read the environment, how to read people.

My grandfather was well known in that part of the country. When he could still see, he had worked in the woods as a log driver and he played the harmonica. I don't know when he went blind but I know that while he never knew what his grandchildren looked like through his eyes, he knew what we looked like through his hands. My first

Sam (Blind Sam) Knockwood

memory of him was of being a toddler and sitting on his knee while he played the harmonica for me and told me stories. I loved that old man. He needed a shave most of the time, but he didn't need a haircut as he was bald — the only Indian man who had a bald head — but that didn't matter. I was always busy talking to him. He could not see the light of day but he could lighten your load of worries by his uncanny way of talking about life as he lived it. The vast amount of knowledge that this man carried with him and shared so freely with me has been with me all my life.

Those times when he would hold me on his knee and sing tunes to me and tell me stories were training for me although I did not recognize it at the time. My only interest then was that he was holding and loving me at the same time. I remember his earlobes were very soft and I would put one thumb in my mouth and grasp his earlobe between my index finger and thumb on the other hand. As I grew older I went from sitting on his knee to standing at his side or sitting next to him, always listening to whatever he was doing at different times of day or night. Often he would be in conversation with older people, and I would sit very quietly as I did not want to be asked to leave the room by my mom. When I talk with people of my generation, they tell me that when they had the opportunity to listen to their elder kin talk, it was the same procedure.

In his younger days, my grandfather played his harmonica for dances. He was a one-man band. When Blind Sam played, everyone listened. I agree with the white man's expression, "He could make that harmonica talk." He wanted his grandson to learn other instruments. He supplied me with three stringed instruments and an accordion.

...learned to play a tune on was the mouth organ,

selling baskets that my mom...

local priest, who asked the price of the basket. My granddad said 50 cents. The priest thought that was a little steep, but my granddad stuck to his guns, saying he "had to make a bit of money on the baskets." The priest asked, "How much did you pay for the basket?" and my granddad said, "Nothing for it." Everyone had a good laugh. The priest bought the basket.

It was a very hard road that my grandfather travelled in his life. While I shared part of that life, I did not know how many hardships he endured. Part of the time that I lived with him was when he went out to make some money for food for his family. Because of his blindness he could not work at any kind of employment. As a result he was given a letter that he could pass out to people on the road. I remember the words on it as if it were today: *To Whom It May Concern. The bearer Sam Knockwood is blind and unable to work. Any assistance that you can render him would be appreciated.*

He would get on the bus or train and travel to a nearby town and walk all day. Sometimes he would go home in the evening or he might stay overnight at a relative's home. I would often go with him all day until the bus or train would bring us back to our home in Newville Lake. But a lot of times we would walk to Parrsboro, nine miles away, and return after walking all day. I would be so tired that I would sometimes have to climb on my granddad's back until I was rested enough, usually a couple of miles, and I would continue walking with him. Sometimes we would be given a drive by someone who recognized us, but there was not very much traffic in those days so as a result we did not hitchhike. When we arrived home my mom would be so happy. We always brought something home for her and my little sister. They were the only ones left at home. Sometimes I would be so tired that I could not stay awake long enough for supper.

All of our conversations were in our own language. It was a very interesting and educational time in my life. As I reflect back on those times today, I see that we did not have very much. But on the other hand, we had the world, our world. We had kinship, love and understanding. There was always someone to listen to us when we talked, but we also learned a lot by listening. Those times were very educational for the young.

My granddad was allowed to travel on the old railway for free. You see he was not always blind. Before he went blind, he worked in the woods. It was an accident in the woods that made him blind. He was a river driver, transporting the logs to a mill site. In those early days, the coal from Springhill was taken to Parrsboro and loaded on the coal boats in the harbour.

July 1st was known as Miner's Picnic day. The picnic was held in Parrsboro at the beach. There were extra trains put on for that day for miners and their families. The extra trains went ahead of the regular trains. On one occasion a few miners missed the special train to Springhill and had to catch the regular train. The conductor of the regular train warned those gentlemen that he would not tolerate any harassment of his passengers or they would be put off the train. Of course, they promised the world so they could get on the train and figured that once the train was moving, there would not be any need to heed the request of the conductor. The train was in the vicinity of Lakelands and Halfway River when the miners decided they would have a little fun. The conductor went to the passenger car that they were travelling on and warned them for the last time. He said that he would stop the train and put them off. The miners let him know that they were going to stay on the train. My grandfather and the conductor were very good friends, and Granddad happened to be on that train

The good conductor came forward to the coach my granddad

little confrontation and how they started the

miner's uprising and help throw them off the train.

Later, when he was blind, my grandfather would arrive home and the trainmen would help him off the train. They would leave him between the rails and he would walk to the crossroad, where my brother and I would meet him. Even after he was blind he was a great walker. He would sometimes walk alone from Maccan to Newville Lake, a distance of approximately eighteen miles. We never heard of him making a wrong turn. When the highway became paved it was easier for him. He told me he would drag his cane along the edge of the pavement as he walked with one foot on the pavement and one on the gravel shoulder.

They talked to us in Mi'kmaq mostly, so as a result I was talking Mi'kmaq pretty well all of the time. My grandfather never spoke English around home unless people came to visit from the community.

My uncle Henry lived next to my granddad. Uncle Henry was married with four children, three girls and a boy. His wife's name was Annie. The three girls were Freda, Ruby and Annie, who was nicknamed Gookie. The boy was Peter. Next to Uncle Henry lived Abraham Gloode and his wife Annie. They had three children, George, Jimmy and Josephine. A short distance beyond my uncle's place were the little church and the community store.

Another of my uncles, Denny, was a big man. He was a bachelor and one day he took me to Amherst. I remember this just as clear as a bell. We came to a restaurant, and he asked, "Are you hungry?" I said, "Not really." He said, "Come on in and have something to eat." He said to the girl, "He hasn't been away from home, so give him something good." So she made up a dish for me. I ate it and he ordered a good meal. She said, "Will you have soup with that, sir." And he asked, "What kind of soup is it?" and she said, "Chicken." He said, "That sounds good." He took the bowl and it was chicken broth. We called the waitress over. She said, "Yes sir?" He said, "Would you take that back to the kitchen? Let the chicken walk through it one more time." She had to bust out laughing too.

Uncle Denny could make anybody laugh. He was a jokester. He was full of fun. He worked in the woods all his life until he became a fireman in the mill. So he always got along well in the white man's world. Of course, he never got into trouble 'cause he was a big man, 200–300 pounds. But could he ever dance, holy shit! He could put those young fellows to shame. He'd step dance. God, he was light on his feet.

A lot of people came to visit at our home when I was young. A lot of Mi'kmaw people came. They worked and lived close by, and there was a lot of camaraderie. I especially remember my uncles coming to visit, Uncle Henry and Uncle Isaac. They always hooked names on us when we were children. My uncle Isaac called me Douglas Way. He would say, "Douglas Way, how are you, Douglas Way." Uncle Isaac was married and had one child. He died early in life. My uncle Isaac lived on Athol Road but he came to visit a lot, usually on Sundays. He sure had a beautiful voice. I did not mind going to church on those Sundays when he was asked to sing in the old Mi'kmaw way. When he would go to church in the town of Parrsboro the priest would ask the choir to relinquish their time that day. My uncle would sing in our own language. Everyone always paid him compliments. Because of Uncle Isaac people always remembered our family.

Uncle John was my favourite uncle. He never spoke English in his life. He was a single man who lived on the Franklin Manor Reserve, in the bush. I would call this man a master craftsman. People would come from many places if they wanted something made. He could duplicate just about anything that was made of wood. Because he

a footpath. It was app————,

not have flashlights. We had lanterns fueled by oil. One night I went with him from our house. My mom let me go. It's strange. I was not afraid. My uncle would stop every now and then to explain some of the nightlife, the winged creatures along with the night crawlers. I was so excited to be travelling in the woods after dark and I enjoyed his company. I remember our walks through the woods and being by the campfire in the evenings. It is this time in life that every young person should have in their book of memories. My fondest memories of this man were sharing those wonderful times with him.

We used to run out onto the bank and watch the buses go by and dream of travelling on them. This one time the guy who was driving said, "Do you want to be a bus driver when you grow up?" and I said, "Yeah," and he said, "You keep watching and you'll learn how to drive." So he took me in the bus and I sat up front. They had the engine in the middle. The bus driver was over here and the big engine was here and there was a seat beside it.

When my sister was old enough, I set up a bus in the bushes a little way from the house. Didn't want to mess up the yard. We had seats. We borrowed chairs from the kitchen. One fellow, Lorrie Rector, came in and he said, "What's this?" I said, "Bus." "That's what I thought it was," he said. That made me feel pretty good. My sister and I used to sit in that. We didn't have much to play with.

Uncle John — John Knockwood, at his cabin in Franklin Manor

Sometimes I drive to Newville Lake from Shubenacadie just for the wonderful memories. I cherish a photo of Uncle John in front of his log cabin on Franklin Manor Reserve, where we spent so many happy hours. I remember how peaceful those days were and I regret the vast amount of history and life stories that I missed because, like the wind, I did not grasp the knowledge as it was being handed down to me by people like my grandfather and Uncle John. This was Indian education from my family being passed from one generation to the next.

My memory of those great men still lingers in my daily living as they were a part of that early childhood education, which I hope will be passed on through these pages, not only to my own offspring but for the rest of the young population of Indian Brook and other communities who need this type of learning to help them be proud of who they are.

Residential School

Shubenacadie Indian Residential School opened in 1930. It was

[text obscured] ... Canada that were funded by the federal

[text obscured]

1996. While the total number of children who died ...
is unknown, Justice Murray Sinclair, the chair of the Truth and
Reconciliation Commission, says that the mortality rate in some
schools was as high as 60 percent. The Shubenacadie school was the
only residential school in the Maritimes. Children from Mi'kmaw,
Maliseet and Passamaquoddy Nations were forced to attend the
school.

Isabelle Knockwood, one of Doug's cousins and a long-time confidant, was a resident at the Shubenacadie school. In her book Out of
the Depths, she records the stories of many of the surviving residents.
Knockwood tells of horrendous abuse of children. At the Truth and
Reconciliation Commission hearings in Halifax, survivors testified that
they witnessed Father Mackey, the director of the school, murder two
young girls by drowning them. Stories of children in the schools being
used for medical experimentation abound. These schools were touted as
educational institutions, but their real purpose was "to kill the Indian in
the child." Douglas Freeman Knockwood is one of the survivors.

Taken Away

My education was cut short as I was taken from my happy home to
a life of turmoil. It was cut off in mid-stream. There was no parting
of the ways from my granddad, no chance to say goodbye to my

spiritual leader and trusted friend. I abruptly went from this life to a life that was very, very cruel.

My brother Ralph was already in residential school. When I was five years old, it was my turn. One day my uncle John and I arrived home and the Mounted Police were at the house. They reached for me saying that I had to go with them. It was a very sad situation as my whole family was at home.

I don't know what happened that day. My dad was working in the woods and he came out for some reason, whether he was sick or what? He was lying down in the bedroom when the Mounties came to pick me up to take me to the residential school. Of course, my mother was all nerved and didn't know what to do and she was crying. She woke Dad up and he said, "What's going on out there?" The Mounties said, "We're taking Freeman Douglas to the residential school. He has to go." My father said, "Oh, no. He's not going to the residential school by Mounties. If he has to go, I'll take him." And they said, "He has to be on the train tomorrow." I remember my dad saying to them, "Don't worry about me." The next morning they were there, sitting across the road when we got on the bus. If I hadn't been on that bus they would have taken me to residential school away from my family. Dad and I took the bus to Maccan to catch the train. Uncle John went back to his camp very lonely and with a heavy heart, blaming himself, saying if he had not brought me home I would not have been taken away. We had a tough time convincing him that it would have happened anyway. For me it was my first trip on the Advocate bus to Maccan. I used to watch the bus as it passed by my door twice a day.

In Maccan we met Susan Hood. She asked my dad if he would take her son Tommy with us and we did. He was a playmate of mine. In that area we all visited each other. It wasn't very far. We walked it sometimes — eighteen miles. The big train arrived in Maccan and we three musketeers boarded the train. Springhill Junction was a fueling stop for coal and water. It was about a twenty-minute stop. And lo and behold my little friend Frankie Pictou came on board. Like the

Shubenacadie Indian Residential School

good gentleman he was, he said that we could all travel together and relieve Mrs. Pictou of the trip. So we had a fun trip to Shubenacadie.

When we got to Shubenacadie we were taken up to the residential school by horse and buggy. When we got to the school they put the run to Dad right away and told him to go back on the train. That was the only time in my young boyhood that I ever saw my dad sad. So Dad went back on the carriage that had brought us up to the school.

My brother, who had already been there for two years, was just over across the way from me. I was happy to see Ralph, but he said, "Don't come over. Don't come near me." He said, "They'll beat you." So I couldn't go and put my arms around him or anything. I was crying. He said again, "Don't come over. They'll beat you." And he kept saying that to me so I didn't go. Later I met him and we talked a little bit. I was younger so I was in a different bracket. He was over across the way from me and I wasn't allowed to talk to him. I wasn't allowed to speak to him. It was the start of a way of life that I had never experienced before. For the next year and a half I was a prisoner. I experienced a lot of abuse both physical and sexual. I couldn't speak a word of English as my dad was never home long enough for us to learn English even though he was fluent in the lingo. My only mode of communication was Mi'kmaq, and I was not allowed to speak in my mother tongue.

I was terrified that first night. I cried and called for my mother. That was the start of many, many nights that I cried myself to sleep. I was devastated. I could not comprehend what I had done, why I could not talk to my brother, my own flesh and blood. I was crying all the time because I was never so alone in my entire life. I always had my mom and my dear grandfather to support me. I cried constantly, and the nuns would slap my hand and sometimes my face.

When we were still living at home, at Christmas time we always had lots of things. Mom and Dad both worked and made baskets. We got along fairly well because Mom always had baskets and if Dad wasn't working in the woods for a lumberman he'd be home helping my uncle John make handcrafts. That's how Dad learned. Uncle John taught him how. And we always had enough food to eat. So Christmas at the residential school was really hard.

Dad came to visit us the first Christmas that I was at the Indian residential school. He arrived with a load of goodies and my brother said we had to eat as fast as we could because they would take them away from us as soon as our dad left. After Dad got a look at what was happening he said he was taking us home. Dad said to Father Mackey, "My children never had snot running out of their noses and into their mouths." He took the goodies back and said to Ralph and me, "Go get your clothes." Ralph said, "We can't do that," and Dad said, "Yes you can." Father Mackey came in and he said, "What do you want to do, break up the family?" And Dad said, "No, I'm taking them both home." Father Mackey said, "No, you're not. You're going home." Father Mackey ordered my dad to leave the premises. Before he left, Dad told Father Mackey that we would be taken out of the residential school. "Mark my word," he said, "my two boys are coming out of this place." Father Mackey just laughed and had the Mounties take Dad to the train station. They took our goodies away as well.

It was at Christmas dinner that I got sick. I had eaten too many goodies and the boys used to play tricks. When they were setting up the tables they would take the shaker, put salt in it and then put the cover on loose. Of course, I was new and everyone was watching. I picked it up and the whole thing went into the turkey dinner. Sister Anderson, a big, red-faced woman, came over. "What's going on here?" she said. The boys were laughing. A pile of salt was sitting on top of my

"God, you were gone a long time." I guess I must have blacked out. When I was allowed back with the general population I was fragile. As a result I was under constant threat. Everyone knew how vulnerable I was. I became the young boy who would not defend himself. As a result, my brother was in a lot of trouble because he defended me constantly. When your peer group can make you do anything and everything at any time, life is not your own anymore. It becomes a way of life without a future.

I did not learn anything at residential school but fear of almost everything. I was afraid to look out the door because I would see nothing that I could understand. I lived in fear of having a bath because we were not allowed to bathe ourselves. As a result, there was a lot of sexual advantages taken on our bodies as we had to bathe in huge bathtubs. Usually there were adolescents doing the bathing. It was a painful ordeal that we had to experience twice a week. We were not allowed to talk about it. Can you picture a five-year-old wondering what he had done to deserve this kind of treatment? At home we may not have had too much material-wise, but we were taught from the old blind man and a very loving mother that there was more to life. There have been reams of paper written about residential schools. I don't have to elaborate, but I want to let you know the vast difference between the school and our original way of life with my loving family.

When my dad went home after that first Christmas, he went to the courthouse in Amherst and opened a case for Knockwood versus the residential school. I have tried to find out but I don't know much about what went on.

Later we came out at vacation time. We came home and I was crying. "You're not going to get us out," I said. My father said, "Don't worry, you're coming out." He said there was a date to release us. We were only back about six weeks, not very long, when we came out. When we were leaving, my father said, "Thank you for your hospitality, Father Mackey. I told you my boys were coming out of here." Father Mackey didn't laugh at him that time. My father won. He beat the system. He was the only Indian to ever take his children out of the residential school through the court system. And he fought the battle himself.

Years later when my wife Kathy was going to Ottawa as part of her job, I said to her, "If you get a chance, see if you can haul out my papers and read them." She came home one night and said, "They didn't think much of your father." And she told me what was in the affidavit.

The stay at the residential school was a living hell. I lived that hell for half of my lifetime, long after I left. I am not proud of that half of my life. After residential school the hurt and the anger did not subside until my mid-life.

Back Home to School and Work

The one-room schoolhouse at Halfway River was built in 1894. One-
~~~~ ~~~~~~ ~~~~~ the rural landscape in Nova Scotia. In these small

Lake was located was called Highway ~~~~. ~~~~
school to the outskirts of the school district — two to three kilometres
— would be within walking distance for children. Both Mi'kmaw and
non-Mi'kmaw children attended the school at Halfway River.

Back with Our Family

My brother and I were happy to be home to renew our love for our family and to meet with the new family that moved into my grand-dad's house across the road from our house. The parents' names were Levi and Susan Pictou. Their children were approximately our age. So our little village of Knockwoods started to expand. Miss Lizzie Paul, her daughter Nancy and granddaughter Mary moved into a building in our yard. So now we had five families staying in close proximity to each other. My grandfather offered his house to the Pictou family, who were having a hard time finding a place to stay in Springhill Junction. When the Pictou family moved in to Granddad's house, Granddad moved in with Mom and Dad.

So we came home to Newville Lake. But the hurt and the anger did not subside. My home life was good and not so good. When we came home my brother Ralph went to live with my blind grandfather.

My brother and I started school at Halfway River. My brother did not get to go to school too long after he came home. One day at school

19

Doug, 7 years old (left), Doug's brother Ralph, 9 years old (right), Doug's sister Marilyn Evelyn (middle), 3 years old

one of the white kids had a new bike, one of the new balloon-tired bikes. Ralph was standing beside it and had his hand on the seat. He was just holding it, looking at it, admiring it. One of the Quinn boys hollered, "Robert, the Indian guy is driving your bike away." Robert came out swinging both hands and he hit Ralph in the chest. You could hear him hit him. Biggest mistake he ever made. Ralph fired away, busting his face open. Blood flew. Robert went home and told his father. My brother was charged with assault. My father once again had his day in court. He defended my brother successfully, got him off the hook on that one. It got to be second nature for Dad to win cases in court. Interestingly, Robert became my friend the third year of school. We were friends into teenagers. He taught me how to drive a car.

After this incident Ralph did not go back to school. Shortly after that he went to work in a lumber mill. So he grew up very fast. He later joined the Armed Forces. At that time the war was on, and my brother got Mom to sign the papers and he was off to war. When he came back from the war, he went to work in the United States.

Robert Smith (on left) and Doug. Robert taught Doug to drive a car.

I started school at the same time as Ralph but I was being taught the very basics as I did not know anything from the residential school except praying and more praying and getting all kinds of abuse both physical and sexual. I did well at the Halfway River school for the first three years. I was taught by three of the most wonderful teachers and ladies. In three years of school these young ladies were able to bring me around to learning the school curriculum. I was able to understand and move forward with a lot of hope and learning abilities. My first teacher was Miss Harrison from Athol. I started grade primary and did grade one with her. My next teacher was Miss Ripley. She led me

Halfway River West School, July 2015

through grades two and three. Then Miss Desmond from Parrsboro taught me grades four and five. These three young ladies brought me from grade primary to grade five in approximately three years. As I look back at those days I realize that these teachers were the foundation for my life. I was able to overcome my fear of going to school for a short while and learned the English language.

My fourth teacher was a catastrophe. I was once again in a crippling situation. This man, who was the brother of the Indian agent, used all the residential school tactics and brought back all the residential school memories. As a result I was back in my shell. I was a ship lost at sea without a rudder or a paddle to move the ship ahead. I spent two wasted years in this man's class. The fear of being taken back to residential school kept me in school learning not a thing. I made every available excuse to stay out of class. He wouldn't let me go to the bathroom so I started peeing myself. Of course, you know how young ~~~ They tease you. So they teased me quite a bit. Finally, I

was a way out of the school boy hindrance to me. I never realized until later how important school was for me. But I was so full of the fears that the residential school held over me. Even at that age in my life those fears that were instilled in me as a little boy were still there. My memories were about a time when I was a lost soul.

After school I stayed in Newville Lake six years, seven years maybe. When I left school, I started to help out with the farmers in the area to get my working skills in order. I worked for a farmer in the Newville Lake area and the lumberman Ernest Harrison. I also worked in the lumber woods. I used to be a yarder.* It was awful. It was okay if I didn't get a wild horse but I wound up with a couple of wild horses that almost took my wrist off. One horse was really bad. When you were hooking up the logs and you'd rattle the chain, he's gone. You had to hook up very slowly. But as soon as he heard the rattle of the chain, didn't make any difference if you had one log or no logs, he's gone. He'd go out to the pile of logs. That's as far as he would go, wouldn't go any farther. But he'd go empty and I'd get pissed off because I had to take him back and hook up again. I didn't know how to swear very well, but I did.

Uncle John also made hockey sticks. He made a hockey stick for me. I was a goalie. God, they were beautiful. And this one he made

---

* A yarder drove the horse that jigged the logs out of the woods.

me was about that thick, about three inches wide. Got me through a lot of games. My uncle John made my sled. The sleds were made for speed. My brother had the fastest sled in Cumberland County. It had those round runners in front and flat ones in the back. That would make them sway, knock people off. Ralph tried to convince our cousin to go for a ride with him on the double runners. He got brave one day and said, "I could sit on it. You'll never swing me off." Ralph says, "Get on." So he got on the back, he crossed his legs and Ralph went down the hill. The front runners were round and he'd dig them in. Then he swung them back the other way and Ralph said, "Ha, ha, ha." I said to the other fellows, "Can I borrow your sled?" "Yeah, go ahead." I followed them down the hill. Ralph was trying to swing him off and my cousin would hang on, laughing to beat hell. They came down about half way and there was a gully. The sled swung sideways and it hit the gully and stopped. They were like flying. I'm coming behind them. My cousin saw me coming and he rolled over on his stomach. He was lucky he'd been thrown into the gully. I went right across his back. When I was going across his body he said, "Jesus!" I will never forget that.

About this time my dad took a job at the coal mine in Springhill Junction, filling the big railway engines with coal. The manager hired Dad on the promise of a house. He told him that he would build him a house to live in if he came to work for him. Dad thought that was really good. We stayed in at Newville Lake for a while. We moved to Springhill Junction when Mom sold the property.

Ernest Harrison wanted to buy the property but Dad said, "No, don't sell it, it is worth more than he has offered you." The property was Granddad's property really. But my mother was in charge of it. She had power of attorney. My mom sold the house. Earnest Harrison came one day when Granddad wasn't home and offered her money for the land. He had offered Granddad money for it before. Granddad said, "It is not for sale. It's for my grandchildren." But when he offered the big money, Mom couldn't say no to money. I can remember the occasion clearly. I was standing there near the tree watching the negotiations. I didn't know what they were saying, but I could hear them talking. I saw him when he reached into his wallet and gave Mom a handful of bills, about ten to twenty dollars. As I got older I realized

with her. "You sold the ...

at him. He knew that she sold the property. Sold it out from under him. When Mom sold the property Harrison moved us all out very quickly. He sent a truck for us to move our belongings the very next day. I think he wanted us out before Dad heard about the sale. So we left Newville Lake at Halfway River and moved to live with Dad in Springhill Junction.

In later years I remember talking about that part of my life with a fellow from the Union of Nova Scotia Indians, a lawyer, I think. He said to me, "You know, you could get money for that?" I said, "Why would I want money for that?" He said, "It belongs to your family. Your mom signed the paper illegally. She wasn't supposed to. Your granddad was supposed to do that."

After Newville Lake

Springhill Junction is the rail siding serving the area around Springhill. It is approximately four kilometres from the coal mining town of Springhill. The Junction was the transportation centre of the Springhill coal mining industry in Cumberland County. The community received its name in 1877 and remained a central hub until the Springhill coal mines closed in 1958. The people who lived in the Springhill area were all connected in some way with the coal mining industry. Life for people connected with mining was hard. The miners worked in an atmosphere of constant danger. Employment was precarious at best, dependent as it was on the ebb and flow of the mining industry. It was from this small working-class town that Doug ventured out into a life beyond his childhood and early years.

Springhill Junction and Beyond

The row between Mom and Granddad over selling the house was so bad that when we went to Springhill Junction, Mom put Granddad in a seniors home in Pugwash. The home in Pugwash was next to an insane asylum and this situation scared Granddad. When Ralph came home from Maine, he wondered where Granddad was. He loved the old man dearly and when he found out where he was, he took him out of the seniors home. Ralph built a little tarpaper shack in Springhill Junction and they moved in there. Ralph put in for a home in Indian Brook and when he got it, he and Granddad moved there.

Dad had a job in the coal mine, and the mine owner provided him with a house. So when we first move there we had a house to live in. Dad's job was a dirty job. He had to stand in the coal dust and make sure that the coal moved along the conveyor belt down the chute to be loaded into the waiting coal cars and into the coal shed. Dad stayed there for a couple of years, but eventually he decided that the coal dust was too much. When he left, he had to give up the house, and we

Brother Ralph home from the army

moved up to Indian Hill. The Indian Hill community was much like reserve land. Years before, it had started out as an Indian community after the president of United Mines in Springhill gave his approval, and as long as Indian people lived on the hill it would be considered a reserve. The houses were pretty well all tarpaper shacks. There was some electricity but no running water.

Out to Work

I started to work wherever I could get work. I worked in construction and on the extra gang on the railroad. I couldn't work too long on the railroad because I was too light. I had to lift big ties and the rails, and my ass was too short to carry them. I could carry but I couldn't raise them up and down. The superintendent said, "You are too little, too short." So he put me on the gravel gang or something like that. I hated it. What I did mostly was carry the water bucket. I had to go to the spring and get a bucketful of water. Then I walked down and gave the guys a drink of fresh water. You had to do that pretty regularly. I did that one summer. Man, was I glad when that was over. At Springhill I didn't work in the coal pits because it was too dirty.

I also did seasonal work in the summertime. Wherever there was a farmer I went working for them. I went picking blueberries. We had to pick the berries into boxes and they had to be clean, no leaves or anything in the berries.

Of course, I was now old enough and I was spreading my wings. I didn't know what it was all about but it was a lot of fun. At this time, I met Bertha, my wife to be, through a friend, Peter Bernard, who was a musician. Peter was going with Bertha's girlfriend, so we ended up going around as a couple of friends. I was 18 and Bertha was 22. It was very difficult because Bertha's mother did not want her around Indian people. When I was working at a garage as a grease monkey night man, Bertha used to come to see me at night. She used to come up when I was working at the garage. One night her mother came to the garage and tore a real strip off me.

When I was 19, Bertha got pregnant with my first boy. I didn't know what to do. Of course, Mom made us get married. That's what you had to do in those days. Bertha moved in with us. When Bernie was born in 1949, I was 20 years old, and Bertha was 24 and she knew what it was all about. She had three sisters. When Carol Ann was born four years later, Bertha and I stayed in a little 12-by-18-foot shack in Springhill Junction. I was travelling around with the boys from the reserve, especially the guys who were drinking wine, rubbing alcohol and whatever we could find as long as it had alcohol in it. Even then I couldn't handle my booze.

I wasn't afraid of work. I did many different types of work but if there was alcohol involved I never finished the job. If I took a drink, all of that crumbled. Just one drink and I was gone. Alcohol took priority over everything else, and my mind could only think of getting more alcohol. At the time I never realized that I was an alcoholic, that I was a sick person.

yelled, "Are you looking for a j...

take a drive. There will be someone here to pick you up." They took us to the farm and we stayed in the house. The old man was good to us. We stayed there until the potatoes were done. They had us back the next year and the year after. Bertha, my wife, went to Maine. We broke her in Indian style.

When we came back home I was tested for tuberculosis. They tested me because of Mother having TB. When they checked me over I didn't have anything.

One day my friend Buddy Brown said, "Why don't we try and get into the regular forces." I was in the reserve army prior to going into active service. There were a lot of people joining up at this time because this was the beginning of the Korean War. We went and joined the reserve army in Springhill. We thought that we could just transfer right into the regular army. At the time the reserves met once a week on Thursdays.

Buddy and I were close in the reserve army in Springhill, and when they called for the recruitment for the 27th Brigade we decided to join the regular army. We went to Truro and went through our basic questionnaire and then we had a medical. My medical came up with a shadow on my lung so they refused me entry and referred me back to health services and put me in the hospital in Springhill. They put me in the hospital for three weeks and tested me for tuberculosis.

But they couldn't find anything. The doctors wrote very strong letters about my health condition saying it was okay. So I went back and was accepted in the 27th Brigade. I was sent to Aldershot for five months of basic training.

Bertha came down to the train to see me off. Our son Bernie was only three, but I could tell that he knew that I was going away. I held him in my arms and when the train started moving I passed him to Bertha and he screamed and cried. As the train started to pull away I stood in the doorway and listened to him screaming. It broke my heart.

At this time our family life was okay. Bertha was getting my army supplement. There was a cheque coming in every month, so she was all right for money. But when I came home on leave she had to hide the money. I would make her tell me where it was hidden. I would take it and just go and get drunk. Alcohol was always available in the army. At Aldershot the wet canteen opened every day at five o'clock and stayed open until eleven-thirty. When it was open that's where I would be. We had draught bear and rum rations and on top of that on paydays we'd go to the liquor store in Kentville. By this time I was drinking anything that had alcohol in it. Once I was drunk I didn't have a care for anybody. I'd get into fights. Sometimes I'd black out. In the army at Aldershot I thought I was just one of the boys. Everyone was drinking and I was just one of the boys. Lots of boys were getting drunk with me but they seemed to be able to get up the next morning for parade without any problem. I had a hard time getting up for parade as alcohol was getting to me more and more. At this time the boys from Aldershot were on draft for the Korean War and were going to Seattle, Washington. I remember there was a rail strike at the time and the recruits were being flown to Seattle on Hercules planes. When my name was called at roll call, they recognized that I was sick in my lungs. I was taken off the draft for Korea and discharged. I went back to Springhill. I was put in the hospital for three weeks where I took all the tests for tuberculosis. But the tests were clear and I was given a clean bill of health. The next year I applied for the army again.

Doug (on right) in Germany, 1951

Because I was in the reserves, I was in the army by six o'clock on the same day. I went to Valcartier, Quebec, for advanced training before we went to Germany.

Again they found a spot on my lungs when we were getting ready to go to Germany, and with the procedure they put me on I wasn't allowed to do anything. I was excused from duty for probably four months while all my friends and buddies were training to go to Germany. During that time I never heard anything about my health.

When Captain Hardy was inspecting for the last round before he sent everyone home on thirty-day embarkation leave prior to going to Germany, he said, "What's the matter with you?" I said, "I don't know, I haven't got clearance from the medics. I don't have clearance to go to Germany." And he said, "Go get your barrack box." Our clothing and all our belongings were in that box. He said, "Take your barrack box and go to headquarters and pick up your embarkation pass." So he wrote out a pass for me and gave me a cheque for me to go home on embarkation leave. So I went home, spent my thirty days, and then came back and went to Germany with the group. We took a steamer to Holland and then a train to Germany. I was there for a year and I took part in all the things there. Bertha stayed back to keep the home fires burning.

Germany

When we arrived in Germany, we weren't allowed out alone. It was just after the war was over, and because of that it wasn't settled yet. There were a lot of the German men, young men, and they hated the ground we walked on. So we had to walk very carefully. We always went to the pubs in groups of two or three. A lot of the basic and advanced training there had been a part of my Aldershot experience. Of course, because I know all my basics, from Aldershot, they promoted me to corporal right away. And I was out doing the drills. I was doing okay with the rifle drill but my voice wouldn't carry. I couldn't make my voice carry for them to hear me, you know. If you were standing from here to that little house over there, you couldn't hear me even if I hollered. And you got 125 men marching. And I'd stand up there and say, "Left wheel, right wheel," and I let them go too far. They couldn't hear me. When I said, "About turn," some of them went left and some of them went right and some of them kept on going. So that put me on the backlist for promotion to a corporal. I stayed as a private.

I stayed in Germany for a year. Married men were only allowed to stay in Germany for one year and single men for two years. When I joined the army I was in the Highlanders. When we got to Germany they transferred us all to the Black Watch. So when I came back I was in the Black Watch. I was repatriated to Aldershot for almost a year, waiting for my battalion to come back from Germany so I could join them. So in the meantime I was a driver. I drove heavy vehicles and in the army I drove buses and trucks, moving buses from Halifax to Aldershot. When I was sober I could do anything I was asked to do.

Doug McAdam Remembers

We were a group of maybe eight to ten motorcyclists. Doug was attached to the North Novies. The big thing we used to do, when we weren't maintaining convoys, was the trips we used to take in the forest. We were travelling around Germany, and we'd do our exercises, hill climbing, river crossing, and we'd get to these unbelievable little "gasthouses" [bars] way back in no man's land.

We were a close group in the Dispatch Riders, and our greatest joy was to go to these gasthouses. Sometimes we were quite inebriated from German beer. But we could take it. Some

equal. I certainly

there was nothing like that. There wasn't too many Indians in the Highland Battalion though. In the Regina Rifles there was quite a few. They were at another camp. We used to get stories.

We were just a bunch of young kids having a ball really. That's what it boiled down to. The only real problem I remember was that we were all sort of jealous of the German police force, which later became the German Army. We used to see them driving around on these beautiful BMW motorbikes; they were 1000ccs. Even the Limeys had their Triumph 500cc twin cylinders. Then here we were, stuck with these bloody Norton 350s from the Second World War! They were hard on your guts, with just one cylinder and you'd have to lean way over them.

After that, I went back and did the accounting for CNR. Other than that we all broke up. Most of the people I knew do not exist now. There's a reunion coming up in Toronto. Doug's the only guy that's left that I know of.

Return from Germany

They opened Gagetown and when my company came back I was aboard to go to Gagetown. It was 1953. In Gagetown we were sleeping in tents on rolled-up mattresses, and it rained for about eleven days steady, and we were all wet, cold and I lost my voice. One morning

Doug (on right) and his dad, Freeman Bernard, when Doug returned from Germany

I couldn't answer my name on parade. They put me in the military hospital. I was there for seven weeks. Finally, they decided to send me to Saint John, to the Lancaster Military Hospital. They took x-rays and the doctor came to my room to report. Now there was probably half a dozen of us who used to play penny ante. We were playing cards when the doctor came down. We were playing penny ante on my bed. The doctor said, "I have good news and bad news. You have an infection in your lung. I guess we're going to be transferring you to Halifax, Camp Hill. You have a case of tuberculosis." The guys playing cards asked, "What is tuberculosis?" The doctor said, "Guys, if I were you, I wouldn't be playing cards with him anymore." One of the guys dropped his cards and money and left.

AND ALCOHOLISM

Fighting Tuberculosis

Tuberculosis (TB) was a common disease until a treatment was discovered in the middle of the twentieth century. It is an infectious disease caused by bacteria. It generally affects the lungs but in some cases can affect other parts of the body. TB, also known as consumption, was virtually untreatable until antibiotics like isoniazid (INH) were discovered. Until that time, surgery to remove part or all of an infected lung was common. Removal of ribs, a procedure called "collapse therapy," was also a common treatment. Ribs were removed in order to collapse an infected lung. As many as seven or eight ribs, usually two or three at a time, were removed. Recovery time for patients involved immobilization for long periods. The disease was most virulent in poor communities. It was particularly active among the Mi'kmaw population. It is estimated that between 30 and 50 percent were affected in some populations. Many infected people died. Those who survived the disease were often left with crippling conditions for which there was no cure. The disease is extremely contagious, being spread from person to person through the air. When a person who is sick with TB coughs, sneezes or speaks, they put TB germs in the air. Other people breathe the germs and may contract the disease.

Leaving Active Service

In November they transferred me to Camp Hill Hospital in Halifax. When I got Christmas leave I went back to Springhill Junction to be at home with Bertha. When I was home I had a hemorrhage. Mom was there to help but it was winter and I couldn't get to the hospital. When the roads cleared, Eddy Wood drove me to the hospital in Amherst. There were four of us in the truck and I was hemorrhaging in a bucket. I was in the hospital in Amherst for ten days when they sent an ambulance to take me to Camp Hill. The hemorrhaging stopped. I was in Camp Hill for a couple of months but they weren't doing anything for me and I got pissed off. I got scared and said, "To hell with this. If I'm going die I might as well die out on the streets because there is no ▨▨▨ for tuberculosis." I knew people who had tuberculosis — Native ▨▨▨ to tuberculosis. I thought if I am

and eve▨▨▨
from me because they knew of my wild beha▨▨▨
behaviours kicked in I got into a lot of fights. I got into a lot of fights with the police force. I felt that they were picking on me all the time and so I defended myself. There were other Mi'kmaw people in the streets but I didn't find them because I was in another alley. I went where I could get money, the money that I could buy booze with. If I met someone who had money, he was my friend until the money ran out. Then I had to find another friend. My friendships were short-lived. If I knew you had money, I became your friend. Wherever you were, I was with you. It didn't make any difference how difficult it was. If there was a mountain there we got over it, together, because you had to have help and I could help you. And because I helped you, I knew that on the other side you're gonna reach in your pocket. So those people I looked out for. I didn't let them out of my sight too far 'cause I never knew when they were going to need help.

One day I was staggering around somewhere. It was in the fall and it was kind of misty and rainy. Then this taxi driver came along. He knew some of my boys and he asked, "Are you looking for a drive to Shubenacadie or Truro?" I said, "Yes." He said, "I am working to twelve o'clock. You go to my apartment and wait for me." I was looking for a drink bad that day. I couldn't find any friends, buddies or criminals. I went to the apartment, he opened it for me, and I went in and he said, "Make yourself a coffee or whatever." So I started to make myself a coffee and I opened a cupboard door where the coffee was and there was a higher shelf above it. I looked up and, my god, it was Christmas Eve and Santa Clause had just landed. Rum, whisky — I'll take this one and this one. I kind of loaded up. Didn't thank him or leave him a note or anything. I don't know where I wound up that night — a hospital or jail? The cops would pick me up and throw me in jail. I probably spent two-thirds of my time in jail because I couldn't pay a fine. I would come up with a drunken charge against me and the judge would ask, "What have you got to say?" I'd say, "Nothing." The judge would say, "Thirty days." It was as simple as that.

One time my dad and I woke up in jail. They picked him up somewhere and picked me up somewhere else. He was in a cell, a big huge one. What do they call it when they put them all together — the old drunk tank? One of the guys said to me, "Have you got enough for a starter?" You know, 25 or 30 cents. One of the boys said, "Hey Knockie!" "What do you want?" "Have you got 30 cents? We've got enough for a bottle." I said, "No I don't have 30 cents." And I made some remark. All at once I heard this familiar voice, "Dougie!" It was my dad. We were in the Truro jail. He was on one side and I was on the other. I said, "You got any money, Dad?" and he said, "Nay." "I'll repay ya," I said. He said, "Nope." Then he said, "I had my last drink. When you wake up in jail with your son, it's time to quit." He never took another drink. When Dad got drunk at home, Mom put him to bed. When he was out on his own, that's when he got into trouble. But when he was at home, we made sure he never got into trouble. So he was protected. Mom protected him.

Then one morning I was sober and I got a job at Kentucky Fried Chicken. It had just opened and I was in on the ground floor. You know, the opportunities in my life were great and I passed them up because of booze. Alcohol did that. So I had this job with Ernie Edwards cooking fried chicken. That's when Kentucky Fried Chicken had the old guy, the white-haired guy, Colonel Sanders. Ernie was the one that taught us. The fat was boiling hot and you had to be careful.

You would drop two chickens in the boiling fat and then snap the cover on. When you got used to it you could do it pretty fast. One day when he was teaching us I dropped the chicken and started to reach down to pick it off the floor. He said, "Leave it there, son. Leave it there.

were going to

were ten stands. So we were making sandwiches for three or four days for the grand opening. We were all filled up and ready to sell those sandwiches. Guess what? It just poured rain. You couldn't walk, it was so bad. It was an opening but we never sold a sandwich. The only sandwiches eaten were the ones we ate. He lost all that money.

Then Ernie opened this big restaurant at the airport. He places the chef and me in the restaurant. It was very extravagant. The chef would send down for twelve steaks — T-bone steaks. In a night he would probably sell eight, so what would you do with the rest. Well they went to the staff and this is what happened every day. Finally, Ernie came to me and asked me if I knew how to work portion control. Usually chefs do that but he asked me, "Would you take over the stores?" I said, "Okay, you're the boss." Whenever the chef ordered steaks he had to get my okay. I had to justify the number of steaks that went out from the stores. So he ordered ten steaks. I didn't say anything and he came back with five. He did that another time and at the end of the week I said, "You know, I'm sorry, chef, I can only let you have so many steaks in the morning. When I come in I will let you have four stakes. You sell the four steaks and send up and I'll let you have four more." He said, "Who's the chef here?" I said, "You are sir, but I am in charge of food."

When I was sober enough, Bertha would let me in to visit Bernie and Carol Ann, but only for a short time. Bertha was living on welfare. She had to hide her money from me so I wouldn't steal it. I arrived once when I was drinking in the daytime. She could smell the booze on me. No entry. All army guys carry a small pack with their gear over their shoulder. She threw it at me when I was going out the door. I caught it and said, "I should throw this back at you." She said, "Go ahead." So I threw it. Caught her in the eye. That was it for me. I had a place in jail to stay that night and for the next four days. They made her appear and threatened to charge me. If she didn't charge me, then I forget what they said they could do. They scared her anyway. I went to the court and of course I didn't know that it wasn't the same judge, but an Aboriginal guy. He said, "I'll let you go this time, but don't come back here and raise trouble again. If you come back and you get into trouble you will be suspended from the army." That was quite a threat. It did sink in. I watched myself when I was walking through Truro.

I had been refused compensation from the army because of my behaviour. At the time I weighed 220–230 and was always into fights. After I walked out of the hospital they ignored me for a while. When they did catch up to me they gave me an ultimatum: take treatment or be forced into treatment. The prosecutor has been through AA (Alcoholics Anonymous). Before they charged me he convinced me to go into court and volunteer to take treatment.

At this time there was a TB tax in Nova Scotia. The tax covered your treatment. If you refused treatment they would send you to jail, because if you were out of jail you would infect the general public. I ran away another time and they sent me to the Kentville "San" for treatment. Bertha and I separated when I went to the sanatorium. She was going with someone else. My daughter, Carol Ann, was born when I was in the sanatorium. Bertha had three or four children after that. They were not my children but even today one of them, Alan, who lives with my grandson, calls me Granddad. One day someone brought him up quickly and said, "That's not your grandfather, you know." Alan said, "He wants to be."

During this stay at Kentville, I met Joyce, a nurse at the hospital. She took a liking to me. But it was not long before I took off again. I was caught again and this time they sent me to the Roseway Sanatorium, just outside Shelburne, Nova Scotia.

you in a cell and locked

None of us opted for the tuberculosis jail. But we were not allowed any privileges because we were flight risks. Because of our past history of running away we couldn't go into Shelburne.

I stayed at Roseway for about a year. I was getting pretty ripe with TB. The doctors told me that I was ready for an operation if I wanted it. I figured I was a dead man anyway so I agreed to have the operation. I was sent back to Kentville and was put on the second floor where the operating rooms were. It was here that they started to cut me up. First, they took my left lung. After this I had to rest for a year, but I didn't heal. Then they decided to take two ribs.

During this time I spent most of my time in bed resting. I was still drinking whenever I could get a little rum and coke. My family did not come to visit because of the cost of travelling to the San. Once, when the doctors though I was dying, Mom and Dad did come to visit.

I used to write to Dad as he was the only one who ever answered me. It was a pleasure to get his letters because he had lovely handwriting and his letters were always comforting. So every Thursday, regular as clockwork, I'd get a letter from Dad with a carton of cigarettes and some girlie magazines. At that time all the magazines showed was a beautiful woman with her dress hiked just about the kneecap. In those days that was sensual. One of the doctors, Dr. Quinlan, knew that I got the girlie magazines from my dad. On Thursdays he would come into my room and say, "Okay Freeman, let's see those magazines." He would sit on the side of my bed looking at women's kneecaps. When I think back it seems strange that they would let me have a carton of cigarettes a week. I guess they thought I was going to die anyway so they didn't bother to take them away.

None of the operations worked. The TB was still in me. It was then that the surgeons decided to try more surgery. This time they took three more ribs. They also scraped the inside of my chest cavity. I was told that this was the last chance for me. I went in for surgery one afternoon. The next morning I heard Dr. Quinlan's voice. It sounded like it was coming from far away. He yelled out my name "Freeman, Freeman." Finally I got enough breath to whisper, "Yes, Dr. Quinlan?" When I opened my eyes I saw the doctors staring at me. Dr. Quinlan said, "He's going to be okay."

After that I was very weak. I could hardly get out of bed. When I went into the San I weighed 237 pounds. After this last operation I was down to 115 pounds. All of the operations had not cured me. I was expected to die. It was then that they started giving this little pill to some of us. The pill was called INH. Within a year all the patients that had taken the pill were much better. A lot of us were going home.

A lot of things happened at the San. I remember this old guy who had been in there for twenty-three years. His name was Mr. Schmidt, from Lunenberg. He used to take all kinds of pills. He would go home and come back. When my friend Donny Gitson was discharged and going home, he says, "What can I get you Doug?" I said, "A quart of rum." And he said, "You got it." But the other guys said to him, "You send it in and they'll take it away." I said, "How?" They told me that they go through everything that comes in. This Cape Bretoner came up with an idea. He said, "Put it in a loaf of bread, they can't trace it." And he was right. I got a parcel in the mail with a loaf of bread, with a big 40-ounce bottle inside. I said to the old fellow who was taking the pill, "You ever have a shot of whiskey?" "Oh god," he said, "a long time ago." I said, "How long is a long time?" He said, "Probably fifteen years." I said, "I got something. I want to give you some." "Give me a mouthful," he said. So I put that much in a glass. Shouldn't have done it. He got sick as a dog. I was sorry. Of course, they were trying to find out what was wrong with him. He said, "Must be something I ate."

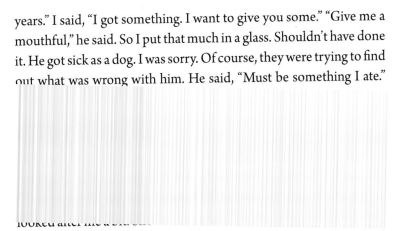

looked after me a bit. She

for a month. When I ran away and was sent to Roseway, we lost track of each other for about a year. While I was gone she went to Halifax but later transferred back to Kentville for a permanent job. When I came back to Kentville for my surgeries, there she was. She was the one that saved my life in the hospital. When she was on the back shift, I never had to worry about pain. She was always there for me. When my light came on she was always the first one in the door. But after a while, people talk. The supervisor was notified that she was answering my call button, so they put her on another floor, took her out of my section.

While I was at the San I lost contact with Bertha and my children. Bertha had gotten custody of Bernie and Carol Ann and was raising them. I felt very alone and thought I was going to die. But there was love between Joyce and me, and it began to build. She was there for me during the three operations, and at the point that I was ready to give up, she nursed me back to health. During those difficult times our relationship developed into a real love affair.

Life was different when I came out of the San. I had been in bed for five years. I couldn't do any of the things I used to do. I couldn't play baseball, hockey or anything. For a year I had to recuperate before I could do any of these things. When I came out, my dad was home by himself in Springhill Junction. My sister Eva had married a guy from

Cohoes in New York State. They had a baby and Mom was staying with them, helping with her grandchild.

For the first year I kept going back to the San. There was a whole support system there and I needed it. During that year Joyce would come and travel with me. She supported me both financially and with her love. I slowly re-gained some of my strength. I did a lot of walking. Because I had no money I was hitchhiking everywhere. If nobody picked me up I just kept walking. I used to walk from Halifax to Windsor. I did get a little work, like dishwashing in restaurants, but that was leading nowhere. In the first couple of years after the San I was drinking heavily. I often got into fights, and I lost most of them. In my mind I was still 235 pounds. I had no power. When I took a swing at someone, they would turn me around, kick me in the butt and send me on my way down the street. At that time I had visiting privileges with the kids, but Bertha did not want me around when I was drinking and that was often. Bertha wasn't drinking at all at this point, just raising the kids by herself.

You know I didn't think I had a drinking problem but I isolated myself from everyone. My relationship with Joyce became quite rocky. I used to call her at all hours of the night. I would plead with her, saying, "I need to talk with you right now." I was very demanding. Joyce suffered a lot because of me. I used to call her up. Many times I would be lying down next to a train track somewhere. I used to drink a lot of rubbing alcohol. We'd mix it up with water until it got cloudy. Then you knew it was good to drink. I'd often be gone drinking for days and Joyce would never know where I was. I was kind of mixed up and she was trying to straighten me out. She was still in love with me. But whenever I got drunk I couldn't go see her. She knew that I was drunk somewhere or in jail but she still put up with me. When I called she would come and pick my carcass up. She'd clean me up and I would go off again. I guess she always hoped that this time would be the last time.

As part of my rehabilitation program from the sanatorium I was eligible to take a course. Because I didn't have a whole lot of education I couldn't go into the higher echelon. What was open for me was a barber or a cook. These trades or professions didn't require a lot of education so that was what was left for me. I said, "I wanted to be a

the old coal stove. I got to

program and he got to know me and he started to like me. He would give me a job to do and it was done. No hesitation, no questions, nothing. And he'd come and look at it and just nod his head. He never paid me a compliment. But you know you done well. His silence was your compliment.

I did this for, I think it was three or four years. But not steady. I would go in for a month, two months, and then I'd leave and get drunk and then go back. And I'd come back in school and the chef would say, "Well, how long are you staying this time?" I would reply, "I dunno." "Get an apron on," was all he said.

When I was sober and working, you couldn't ask for a better man to do the job and it was the same way with cooking. I started to learn how to cook, got a chance to learn how to operate a kitchen, set up and take down a banquet. I learned all of that in no time at all. When I got sober it would work like a charm. As a result, the chef always put me in charge. He had a contract with the Bedford Yacht Club and he used to get contracts for dinners for six to ten. Couldn't take any more than ten because it would go into a different class. It was lots of money for him. He had one guy that was with him for two years. Did all the work. That guy left and two weeks later this man came in looking for a banquet. When the guy left, the boss called me to the office and said, "I'm going to send you out with the boys tonight. I'll go down and show you how things operate and then I'm going to leave you to put it together. I'll be back fifteen minutes before serving time. You're in charge of the guys. They know this." This was my first assignment on my own. And it's a good thing I was sober when I did that because it was a lot of work. But I did it, and I did everything in order. He came down and checked it all over and he said, "Look at that. Get the right person in the right place at the right time. You don't even have to check it over." And he went to the other guys and he asked, "How did you find working with him?" "No problem," they replied. "If we didn't know something, he showed us how to do it." Chef took a liking to me and that's what my job was for the next year, when I was sober. When I left, I got the little piece of paper that said I graduated. I was a cook. The chef told me, "Any time you get a job, if you need a write-up, let me know." I did get one when I went to the States.

The cooking course, paid for by the government, was a six-month course. It took me three years to get there. But it was to the chef's advantage too, because he didn't have to worry about the banquets at the Yacht Club. He would tell me who was captain and he'd give me the menu and six men and we'd go down and set it together. We were getting the next day off and half a day the next day. Which was okay. Didn't make a hell of a lot of money but it was nice to get the time off.

I went to Toronto after the cooking course. In Toronto I was really into drinking bad. Joyce called me up to say she had got a leave of absence from her job in Kentville to do a graduate degree in nursing in Montreal. She said, "I have an opening in Montreal." But she said, "I can't go without you. I don't know how you are but I would like to see you before we go away together." So I came home. Finally she got me settled down enough to go with her to Montreal, where she went to get her degree in nursing.

I worked as a cook there. I worked in the Army–Navy–Air Force of all places. I was just as free as I could be and I didn't drink a lot. I mostly stayed sober until she got her degree. She knew these girls that were in the course with her and of course they got to know me. We used to have visits and have dinner together. I tried not to drink. It ~~~d job for me to totally stop but I stopped to the point where ~~~ the bottle and won. When we

was into the ~~~

I caused a ruckus and Joyce got fired. ~~~ because of me." After Kentville Joyce stayed with her mother and got a job in Truro. You know, I was kind of mixed up and she was trying to straighten me out. But I was getting worse all the time. Joyce, much as she loved me, her love wasn't strong enough. It should have helped me. The booze, I loved the booze. It is a funny thing. When I was sober I would do anything. And when I was drinking you couldn't make me do a thing.

During this time I only had contact with my children when Joyce gave me money to take one of them out for a night or a day. She was the one that kept us together. She said, "That money's only for the children." She would pick Bernie up and put him on the bus and I'd pick him up in Halifax, where I was working. But one thing I was guilty of. I didn't let him stay the full amount. If his mother let him go for four days I would always sent him home after three. He must have been hurt, you know.

Meanwhile that little piece of paper I had qualified me to get a dishwashing job down in Cornwallis naval base. They made me a pot washer. That was not so good after being drunk the night before.

I was really getting into the booze, the heavy part of it when I got a letter from Joyce. A woman who she had met when she was in Montreal was now a supervisor in Saskatoon said she had a job for both of us. She said that there was a job for a nursing instructor coordinator for the province of Saskatchewan. It was a big deal. There was another position in the hospital, a cooking job.

When we got together, she said, "Only one of us is going." And I said, "Okay." That was the hardest time I think in my life. The day we parted, she was driving the Volkswagen that we had, she said, "I will drive you somewhere." I said, "No, it's okay." She drove away crying and I guess I did the same too. I went to Mom's in Springhill to visit for three or four days. Afterwards when I was hitchhiking back to Truro, there was a clump of trees just outside of Truro. I don't know whatever made me do it but I walked across the road and I went into this bunch of alders. You couldn't see me but I could see the traffic. Just as I got into the alders I turned around and I saw her driving by. That was the last time I saw her. I guess it was supposed to be. I never heard from her until I was in Yellowknife years later. I met her sister. I didn't know it was her sister. She was a cashier in a grocery store.

After Joyce, my world sort of crumbled. I crumbled with a bottle of wine. There was a long time coming back from that fall. When I was drunk I was a mean sonofabitch. You know, if I walked down the road and I didn't like you and if you stayed on my side, you'd get a punch in the mouth, or a kick in the nuts, or whatever. There was one thing my father did for me — he taught me protection. He was good with his hands, fast with his hands. I used to put the gloves on and he'd pound me around the ears and my head.

After Joyce left I mostly lived in Halifax but I did travel around some. I did go to Montreal a couple of times and to Toronto once. I also went to Prince Edward Island to pick potatoes. I went on my own. I didn't know my way could be paid. I hitchhiked over and then I got a job with this farm outside of where the ferry stops. Borden. A guy came and took me home. I went with his boy and when I got to their farm there was three other potato pickers. It rained, I think, after we were there, three or four days anyway, it rained. We all went to Summerside. "We picked potatoes the next day and he paid me $1.40."

"I don't know how it happened but I ended up in Tignish one

weekend. I was supposed to be back to pick potatoes on Monday. So we get on that train that comes up the back way. It conked out. The engineer said, "We'll be going in another ten, fifteen minutes." I ⟨…⟩ So I'm walking along, taking a swig ⟨…⟩

⟨…⟩

It's ⟨…⟩

"Let's try it." I took it out and gave it to ⟨…⟩ a hooker. The fireman didn't take any but the engineer took a hell of a good swig.

The train took me into Summerside and of course I had this jug and trying to get rid of it. I couldn't get anybody to help me in drinking it. I had to drink it myself and I got drunk. So they put me in lockup to get sober again. Next morning, they let me go out. I was back on the train crossing the ferry to go back to Nova Scotia. They used to put the train cars on the track on the boat. They were pushing passenger cars and the engineer spotted me. I'm standing in the doorway and he said, "Got anything left in the jug?" I said, "No, they took it away from me." He said, "We could have used it this morning."

Except for my little trips, I lived on the streets of Halifax pretty well all of the time. I did everything I could to get money to buy liquor. I stole it and I begged for it. I did not openly bum money. I did it sort of on the side. I'd talk to people and get to know them and tell them the hard luck story. They'd reach into their pocket before they walked away and they'd give me whatever. I did very, very good at that. I had a fair amount of lies to tell. I'd fib everything. Never told the truth. If I asked for money and you didn't give it to me and I knew you had it, then you were in trouble. I didn't hesitate to take it. Then I would go to jail. I spent a lot of time in jail. The police knew me. They'd see me and they'd book me into the local jail — six days, then ten days, then they moved it up to thirty days. I did a lot of thirty days in the Halifax jail — the old one with the bars and the concrete. A dismal place.

I didn't get booze when I was in jail. It was too close there, very crowded in the cell, just room for a double bunk, one on top of the other. A lot of times very severe beatings happened in those cells. If the guy in your cell didn't like you, you had to try to protect yourself. A lot of guys passed away in there because they were too drunk and couldn't handle themselves. You didn't hear too much of that but that's the way it was. I'd live there, come out, go back again, get caught on the street, go back in again. It was a bum's life, really. I didn't think I'd ever come out of there. Wherever there was a hole in the wall, I went in, and where there was a free handout, I went. And I only had one lung. Got sick a few times. I never thought about how sick I was. I'd go and get drunk and go to jail, lie in cold bunks. Things I never thought I'd do but I did. Never thought that I'd go and steal food but I did. I was hurting people. It was a hard and lonely life. Then I started going to AA.

I didn't know anything about AA. I was drunk for a week or something and I was sick, had no place to go. And someone on the street said to me, "Join Alcoholics Anonymous." I asked, "You know where it is?" "Yeah," he said, "up on Dresden Row." That night I stayed drunk until one o'clock or whatever, so then at two o'clock I found my way to this Easy Does It (EDI) club.** I knocked on the door and this fellow came to the door and said, "There's nobody here right now." He was the caretaker cleaning up the place. "But," he said, "there's somebody here at eight o'clock. You come back at eight o'clock." And I said, "Okay." I went to my favourite place, the local police station. At the jail they let you stay overnight but they kick you out in the morning. So I stayed there, and the next morning I was up at that clubhouse at seven o'clock, waiting — cold, hungry, sick. Finally, a guy came along and opened the door. He said, "Are you looking to come in

---

** The EDI club was a gathering place where alcoholics and recovering alcoholics met to socialize.

here?" And I said, "If I can." He said, "Come on. Come in with me."
So he took me in.

The daily program was run by a fellowship of men and women
~~~~~~~~~~~~~~~~~~~~ They had a meeting at certain places,

one of the founding members ~~ ~~~ ~~~~~~~
kept hollering, "Who's going to take him?" They were going to the
meeting, every one of them, but they didn't want to take me. When
Bruce came though the door a few minutes later they said, "Bruce,
who's going to take this guy to the meeting?" He looked around and
must have been thinking, "What the hell's the matter with you guys?"
But he said nothing. He asked, "Nobody going over there?" "Yeah,"
they said, "but the car's filled up." Just then this man came through the
door and said, "Hi Bruce." Bruce said, "Are you going to the meeting
tonight?" He said, "Yeah." So Bruce said, "Do you mind taking this
fellow?" He said, "Not a bit." I never knew that guy's name. He took
me to my very first meeting. He took me over there. I walked up those
long flights of stairs at the old Dartmouth fire hall. Man, they were
long. Coming off a drunk I was dizzy just walking. I had to walk up
those flights of stairs but I made it. And when I got up there a little guy
opened the door. He said, "God, I am glad to see you." Nobody ever
said that to me. He asked me to go and have coffee. I said, "This man
brought me over and I think I'll go with him. I'll be over tomorrow."
He said, "You sure?" I said, "Yeah." "You won't pick up a drink first?"
he asked. So they were very supportive of me not drinking.

While going to AA I worked in many places as a short-order cook. I
tried to get a job as a cook but they wouldn't hire me as a cook. Nobody
would hire me as a cook. So at this time AA was on the outskirts.

Then I went to New Brunswick but the same thing happened. The last place I worked there was at the University of New Brunswick. I worked as a cook's helper, just a Joe boy washing pots and pans and mixing up different things. The guy I worked with said, "You just stay with us and you'll be a second cook before long." But I left because I couldn't get anywhere past second cook. I had the qualifications to do a chef's work and I knew that. So when I couldn't go any higher I said, "To hell with this." I got my pay on a Friday or Saturday, and I got my clothes cleaned up and I said, "I'm going to Boston." Everybody said, "Hey, have a good time in Boston." So I packed up and I bought a ticket for Boston. For me Boston was just a place to go.

I started drinking on the bus. I left Tuesday and I arrived in Boston on Saturday morning. Now, where I stopped in between I don't know. But anyways, I made it. I was standing on the street and I said, "Where the hell am I?" I looked around and I didn't recognize anybody. And the people going by, they were talking in a different lingo and I said, "Jesus, I pulled a dandy this time." And I looked around and I said, "I better go and see if I can get my way back to Nova Scotia." So I started to walk around and I see the signs on the window, "Short-Order Cook," "Cook's Helper," all kinds of signs for cooking and I said, "Geez, I'll get a job here." So I did. I took this job across the way at a hotel, breakfast cook they wanted, and I said, "Oh shit, nothing to that." Of course, I just come off a drunk and this was something to do after a drunk.

They ordered bacon and eggs and toast and everything. From the time I went in at ten after nine until the time I left at ten after two, that's what I made: bacon and eggs, omelets and everything. All breakfast. And the place was full. When I got out of there, sweat was pouring off me and I didn't have any money for a drink. Anyway, I got out and met a couple of boys from home, took me in a tavern and we sit there and talk and I said, "You know, I got some money coming to me. I worked all day." "Why don't you go and get it?" When I tried to get it they wouldn't give it to me, locked me out.

The next morning I started to go back, and I said, "What the hell I want to go in, beat my ass off, all for nothing." I stood there. All at once I heard my name called. I looked around. I thought, oh shit, I ~~~ ~~ ~~~~ The angels are calling me. I could hear this voice,

coming through, and it kept ~~~~~~ ~ coming through there." And sure enough I stood there long enough and a man's body started to come out. It was a guy from Truro reserve coming across the street. I said, "My god, am I ever glad to see you."

We talked a while. "My god, are you sick? You're so sick." And he reached in his pocket and had a little bottle of muscatel wine. It was 70 cents, the bottle. He said, "Drink all of it." That's how bad I looked. We stood there talking for a while, putting two great minds together to make $5. He asked me if I had any money. I said, "No." I was going through my coat pocket and hauled out an empty bankbook. He said, "Doug, do you got money?" I said, "No there's nothing in that account." He said, "Write me a cheque." "What?" "Write me a cheque," he said. "Write on the bottom, 'paid in American funds.'" I said okay and 15 dollars I put down. It wasn't too heavy. He was gone five minutes and came back with 15 dollars. And we had a party. We came back that afternoon for some more and we went on a party for I think two or three weeks.

I started getting sick and couldn't make it back to Halifax. One morning with all these goodies, a shopping bag here, shopping bag there, then I saw this little sign above the door on Dover Street, "Twelve-Step Recovery House." I looked up and I said, "I gotta go in there. Not today." So I went down and drank up our booze, and that's when I started to get sick, and a week later I don't know how I wound up at that door. I knocked on the door and a little short guy came to the door and said, "Holy shit, am I ever glad to see you. Come on in. Come on in. Sit down over here." He went and got a coffee. "Where are you from?" and I told him Nova Scotia. "Oh my god." Anyway, he babied me as long as he could, and a couple more guys came in and they took over and when suppertime came there were twelve or thirteen of them. Then the boss came home. "You can't keep him here. He gotta go somewhere. He's too sick. Take him to a detox centre." A couple of guys got a taxi and took me to Walpole Street prison. They had a detox centre down there. On the one side of it was the rehab centre for alcoholics and on the other side of it there was the cells for criminals. They were waiting to be sentenced.

That's where I went and I stayed there for nine days or something. I had the last room on the corner down at the end, and this fellow on the other side said, "You're new! How are you feeling?" "Well I'm getting around," I said. "That's good," he said. "You know, those people who brought you here, you listen to them when you leave. They'll treat you okay." There was a partition all the way up. We talked for a while through the partition and then he said, "Do you smoke?" "Yes." "Do you have any?" "No." "I got a box. Watch this. I'm going to send you a pack of smokes. They should bounce close to your cell." He shot it out and it hit the wall and bounced back on my side and I said, "Oh, I thank you very much." We got talking together and about the second or third day one of the guys came down and seen me with some smokes and I said, "I'm doing okay. I'm coming back to the centre. I'm doing okay." He said, "Where are you getting your cigarettes?" "Next door." "I'll tell you a story when you come out."

So, I think Friday or Saturday, he took me back to the halfway house. They had a meeting, an AA meeting, every night. You had to go to one, that was the criteria. I got in and it was suppertime and we were eating and the boys were speaking about their experiences of going to the state hospital. I was no different and I mouthed off about this and that and I said, "You know I didn't have any cigarettes

when I went in there, but the guy in the next cell got some for me."
They said, "Albert DeSalvo," and I said, "I don't know who he was."
"That was your killer friend," they said. I said, "No. Didn't sound like
a killer." They told me he killed a lot of people, seven or eight. Albert

He was drinking

I got an apartment and I had my money in the bank. That's where I
started my sobriety, up there, and I haven't had a drink since. I was
34 years old. Once I got sober and I started to learn about the pitfalls
of alcoholic drinking, it just started to register. I still follow the AA
program today. One drink and I'm gone again.

Patsy
I used to make trips home on weekends and holidays as often as I
could. On one of my trips home when I was still drinking I met Patsy.
I found a friendship with her family, the Morris family, through Dad
when he was boarding with them. Then Dad moved back to Springhill
Junction to the old homestead. I used to go down there and do a little
work for them. I sort of had a place to stay when I came home from
Boston. That's how the relationship with Patsy developed. Mrs. Morris
wanted Patsy to come with me to Boston. Patsy got a job as a hotel
waitress. In about a year she got pregnant with Joey. That sort of cut
the working time for her. So she stayed home. When Joey was born
she went back to Nova Scotia.

After I got sober Bertha gave me custody of the kids. By this time
she had three other children, including Alan. When I got custody I had
no place to put the children so I had to send them to the residential
school. When they were in residential school I used to come to Nova

Scotia to visit once or twice a month. After a few years Mrs. Morris told me that she would look after the children so I took them out of residential school and they went to live with the Morris family. That was a very good arrangement both for me and the children.

When they came out of residential school they used to come to live with me in Boston for the summer. I was going to AA, so then they were okay because Bertha would let them go to work with me because she knew I wasn't drinking. They both travelled together and went back and forth the first year. When I was first in Boston I got a few short-term jobs. I worked at Boston University and I worked at the airport cafeteria and then at Brighton cafeteria. One day I met this fellow and was having a coffee. He said, "Where do you live?" I said, "Nova Scotia." "Wow," he said, "you're a long ways from home." And I said, "Well, I had to get the hell out." "Why?" he asked. I told him, "I couldn't get a job." He asked me, "What do you do?" "I'm a cook," said I. "Oh jeez," he replied, "I got a job for you. Come on over tomorrow morning." I asked, "Where?" "Leslie College," he said, "I'll tell the boss you're coming over. We need a cook."

So I went to Leslie College the next day and they hired me. I got sobered up of course before I went there, and I went and stayed for three months. One day the superintendent came to me to tell me, "You know after three months, we usually hire people for full time. If you are interested we'll make you full time." I said I was interested so they made me full time. Then he said, "You know that you will not be cooking full time. You'll be cooking a bit here and a bit there. But you'll be here for the school season, at Leslie College for girls." So that's where I stayed. When summertime came all the other guys would be going on holidays, right, but I didn't go on holidays because we weren't part of the school system. When the first or middle of May came, universities and colleges were quitting and everybody was going home. So what they were doing was filling in for vacationers. So I would wind up going wherever they sent me. That's what I did, I loved it. Of course, I got along well with management. In no time at all I was going up to the mountains in Vermont. There was a place up there where they started cooking turkey months before thanksgiving. They'd cook them and they'd freeze them because there were so many people coming in they couldn't cook all of the turkeys at once.

the locations that we found ourselves in. We tended to move — not a lot — but more than usual. My earliest recollection was in Springhill Junction. We lived there when I was just a youngster and I have snippets of memories of my dad coming home. He was in the army then — I knew there was something special because he had these special clothes on. I remember an incident of him trying to teach my mom how to drive and my mom drove the car into a snowbank and snow was flying everywhere.

Another incident I remember was when he was returning home from Germany. There was a big convoy of vehicles leaving Springhill Junction and going to, I guess, the base in Springhill. I can remember standing on the side of the road seeing all these vehicles going by and waving and hoping to see Dad but everybody was dressed the same and I was wavin' at everybody. Dad said he saw me. He says he almost fell out of the truck wavin' at me. And Mom — I went up and I saw Mom and I said, "I don't know if Dad saw me or not. I was out there wavin." Even my hand got tired. But Dad said every man in that convoy waved at me when they went by. I remember him coming home that night and there was all kinds of happiness in the house. Those are some of the snippets that I recall from the early times and then some of the bad times you tend to forget or bury and you don't wanna remember them. All I remember is something happening and next thing you know I was — we had to move from there, move in with a friend of Mom's and we were there for a while.

We never had our own place until later on. We lived with other people and it didn't give you much sense of place and security. You're always there at the good wishes of another person. If anything went wrong it was usually your fault. Then after — when my mom got sick with tuberculosis and Grampy and Granny couldn't look after us, we wound up going to the residential school. We had no place else to go. I stayed there until I was 16 — that was about six years. The year I left was the year before they closed it down. My sister left the following year. That was a traumatic time — Dad would show up once in a while — he was working in Halifax — and take us out for the day and it was nice. It's just that at the end of the day you knew you had to go back there and it was terrible. It was the same with going home at Christmas time. Go home at Christmas time and it's all — everybody's happy and the day comes you have to go back and that was the worst part about it. There's all kinds of things that go through your mind when you're going back to some place like that.

When I left the residential school I went to live with the Morrises in Middleton. It was nice. She was a kind person and never made any demands other than to keep my room clean. She would do my laundry for me and she would cook and things like that. She treated me well. I have no complaints about that. Carol Ann came a year later. She only stayed there for about a year and she went back and stayed with Mom in Springhill. She graduated from high school in Springhill — the first Mi'kmaw woman to do so.

I finished vocational school while I was at the Morrises. The first year I was in vocational school Dad came and asked me to go to Boston and I went to Boston with him and got a job working as a potwalloper in the kitchen. Dad was working as a cook and I was working at dishwashing and mopping the floors

all of his cigarettes.

go to the Red Sox games and she would whistle and we'd be up there, boy comin' back with sunburnt tonsils.

When we were there Dad was going to AA and he took me over a couple of times on Saturday mornings to just basically hang with him at the AA hall. And I remember they had a real nice pool table in there. Never played pool at all in my life. And I was sittin' there lookin' at it and this guy says, "C'mon, I'll show you how to play pool." And I said, "Okay." So he racked them up and he explained the game and ya gotta sink your balls in and stuff like that. And I said, "Okay." So, after I got the basics down he says, "Okay, now we're gonna play." Cleaned the table with me! And I sat there and I looked at him and I said, "Well, that wasn't any fun!" "Rule number one," he says, "don't play with anybody better than yourself." Dad was sittin' there and he's lookin' at me and he says, "I don't even play with him because he's too good."

We got to know a lot of people in the AA group and I always tell people whenever I'm at the AA meetings or Dad has an anniversary, I always say that if it wasn't for AA, we wouldn't be here. There would be no Dad. There would be no anniversaries or anything, y'know. But, I can't say enough about AA. It's one of those things that helps you to regain your life and try to patch it together again if you want to.

My mom — when we were growing up — she never once told us not to love our father. And she was always, y'know, whenever Dad showed up she was always very nice to him and she expected us to be nice to him too. And I think that goes a long way with us re-uniting with Dad again in a positive way. And y'know, I always told Mom that I was thankful that she never said anything bad about Dad. She said, "Well, I knew that it wasn't him. It was the alcohol. I knew he was a good man inside." That helped us a lot, like I said y'know, after going through residential school and all the crap that we had to go through there, and then meeting up with Dad again and having a second chance, as it were. And that was really, really nice, y' know. That would be the high point in our life in terms of re-connecting and coming together as a family again. And, we just branched out from there and we had lots of trips — we had our AA family in Boston and then we had our AA family in Springhill and Dad would bring a carload down from Boston and they would have a meeting and everybody just — it was beautiful. It was really, really nice. They were re-connecting and they said, "Well, we're gonna come to Boston," and Dad said, "Yeah! That would be great!" So, the group from Springhill come down. We'd fill up the ole Falcon station wagon and they'd fill up one of their cars and we'd head across the border. They would stay a week or a couple o' days down there and everybody had some place to stay and it was really nice that we were able to make those connections between the two groups. And it formed a bond up until the last old member passed away — it was a special time. And I was really privileged to be part of that and travel with them and laugh with them and got to know them and a lot of the people from Springhill knew me as a little ankle biter and they'd say, "We remember you when you were just so big."

During the last year that I was in Boston I worked at General Electric in their small jet engine division. When I came back

Recovery

Alcoholism is a disease. It is a condition in which a person becomes

...understanding of the disease that allows him to work with alco-
...victims to successfully bring them back from the brink of despair.
...became one of the most sought-after alcohol and drug addiction
...nsellors in the country. The story of how he set up detox and treat-
...t centres across the country — in the Maritimes, in Montreal, in
...wknife, in Edmonton and elsewhere — is a testament to his inner
...th, a strength that his son Bernie and daughter Carol Ann always
...was there.
...While he worked a lot with Indigenous people, he also did much of
...rk with non-Indigenous people. Doug explains that an alcoholic
...coholic, whether Indigenous or not. In either case he works to
...dignity and self-respect, essential elements in the successful recov-
...alcoholism.

...ife in Boston

...re very good in Boston. I was working at Leslie College. They
...y salary, then they gave me a boost on top of my salary, then
...me expenses for travelling back and forth. If I stayed there
...or my hotel, my meals. I was doing good.

...was working at Leslie College, I did a lot of volunteer work
...s in the prison and the rehab centres. I used to go to do
...ork all the time. On weekends I would go somewhere

from Boston I was working in Amherst at Bob's Engineering. Dad had come back and he was working for the Union of Nova Scotia Indians. He was going to all those reserves and trying to get people to stop drinking and go back to school. He came to

I went down and went in and asked for my high school marks. I can remember just as clear as if it were yesterday. The guidance counsellor looked at me and said, "What do you want your high school marks for?" I said, "I am applying to Sir George Williams University." She says, "They'll never take you. You don't have the marks for it." "Well I don't know about that," I said, "but I'd like to have them." The next thing you know I got accepted at Sir George Williams University. And there I am in the most cosmopolitan city I'd ever seen.

When Dad talks to people there's that innate understanding that he knows where he's coming from and he's coming from the same place they are. And that place that he's coming from is not only a combination of knowing who he is as a person but also his life experiences that he's, more or less, been forced to learn over the years — just by mere circumstances. And there are times when I listen to him, and he's talking, and I listen and — the way he tells a story and the way I tell a story is the same because my grandfather taught me how to tell the same stories. And I don't have the same impact that he does but — that's because of his experience and things like that. And I can tell you one thing though — I'm really proud of my Dad. I'm totally amazed that after all these years and all the things that he's gone through, and all the things that I've gone through, and my sister, and all of us — that we can still come together and still be a loving family. And we're not tearing at each other and saying you did this, you did that, why did you do this, why did you do that. And those are some of the issues that we have come to terms with in our own life and we've settled them and now we're there for each other and we're not there to — because we know the pain of not being there for somebody. And I'm really glad that Dad is — he's my Dad. That's all I can say.

PART THREE

A NEW LIFE, A NEW CAREE

*an
hol
He
cou
men
Yello
streng
knew*

*W
his wo
is an al
restore
ery from*

A New

Things w
paid me n
they paid
they paid
While I
with addict
volunteer w

and do volunteer work. In fact the group I belonged to in Chelsea
came to put a meeting on in Springhill. So when I started getting the
meetings going, we exchanged meetings. I came home and one of
_____ _____ said, "Why don't you get us a commitment? Put the

single guys they went to different ___

When they were in Boston, the kids used to come with me to
meetings, and they also went to the Alateen meetings, which are for
children of alcoholics and drug addicts. So that's how they started to
learn about alcohol and drugs. They were able to help one another. I
got custody of my two kids and I was able to bring them over every
summer. Bernie came first. He worked with me for two summers
but had to come back to go to school. Carol Ann had another year of
school. Then she came to work with me. They both started out in the
cooking field. Bernie used to love it 'cause there were a lot of young
girls. Of course, he was a nice looking man. The girls would always
find some excuse to go and talk to him. Of course, Carol Ann was a
knockout anyway. I used to take them to the ball game, Red Sox ball
game. I don't know where she learned that one-fingered whistle, but
outside, jeez, it'd tear your eardrums right out. I took her to a ball
game one Saturday afternoon and her little friend came with her. We
were sitting there and all at once two little boys almost broke their
father's arm off. "Daddy, daddy, look at that girl whistling!" She was
there with her fingers. That was her fun. People never thought that
nice, mild-looking little girl would have that type of strong whistle.

When Bernie graduated from grade twelve, he took a trade in weld-
ing. Man, he was good. He came to work at Revere Beach. I forgot
the name of the outfit but he was there for three years, in Chelsea,

Massachusetts. He was making money like you wouldn't believe. So they both started out working for me and then they branched off.

Bernie got so afraid they were going to scoop him for the army. All his buddies had been gone for two years. He said, "I guess I'll go home, Dad." "What are you going home for?" I asked, "You'll never make this kind of money in Nova Scotia." "I know," replied Bernie, "but I could be put in the army here." "They won't touch you," I said, "You're a Canadian citizen. You don't have to worry about that shit here." But I couldn't convince him. He went home.

Carol Ann went back to live with her mother when she was in grade twelve. She was the first female Mi'kmaq in Nova Scotia to graduate from high school.

Carol Ann Remembers

What I remember about my dad, from when I was a little girl, is what my mom told me. He was in the army and he'd gotten tuberculosis, and he was in the hospital for about five years. He used to bust out of the hospital every once in a while. This one time, I gather, he wanted to see us, and he came to see me, but the cops arrived, got him and took him back to the hospital.

A little while later I caught TB. I was in the hospital for about two years from the time I was eight months old until I was two years old. Dad got to know the nurses in the sanatorium and they would tell him how I was doing. He'd get them to come and take me out for a little bit.

When I was finally allowed to come home, I don't remember Dad too much because my mom wouldn't let him see us when he was drinking. But I'd always know he was there. I'd wake up and there'd be a snowsuit there or there'd be a doll he'd left, or something like that. He used to come sometimes at night, so that's mostly how I knew him.

I think that our relationship was always there, even though he wasn't around much at first. When I did see him, Dad always made me feel like I was the most special person in the world. So I just idolized him. Every once in a while, Mom would allow Bernie and I to go out with him. He'd have candy and stuff like ~~~~~ ~~ ~~~ ~~~~ ~~ him it was just like Christmas

would talk about her time with Dad at times, but Mom really loved him.

She would tell me about the dates that they went on. They used to hop the train to Springhill. Or they'd take the pushcart. She used to tell me that they'd meet by an old bridge at Springhill Junction. And they'd meet and make a lean-to in the back of the woods. She said, "I always liked the smell of spruce!"

She used to tell us how, when she and Dad were going to get married, she was already pregnant. And in those days you didn't have a baby without a husband. Anyway, Mom wasn't 21 yet and that was the age of maturity. Her father wouldn't sign for her to get married. Her mother wouldn't sign for her either. So Mom told her mother that if she didn't marry him she was going to throw herself in front of a train! My grandmother told her that she would rather see her dead than marry an Indian.

So Mom waited until she was 21. She turned 21 in July and Bernie was born that September. So you can imagine her walking up the aisle with Dad, with her tummy all huge! She told me about their honeymoon. She told me that during their honeymoon, Dad wound up playing in this baseball game and there she was, sitting on the ground watching him play baseball.

Her and Dad and Grampy and Granny were living in a tarpaper shack, and they built an extension for their bed. And

Mom would tell me that it was so cold that at night when they got into their bed their bodies would actually thaw the mattress. But she said she loved it! She was cold but she said she loved it.

Mom used to tell me that when Bernie was born his hair was blond and that he used to rub his head against Dad's head so that his hair would turn black! She would talk about when Dad was in the army and serving overseas. She had a picture of Dad. And every night Bernie would have to kiss the picture goodnight and put it underneath his pillow.

My other grandmother, Dad's mom, always called her "Dus," because she always thought of her as her daughter. Even when Dad and Mom got divorced, Granny told her, "You'll always be my daughter." Mom and her were very, very close, right until the end of Granny's life. Whenever Granny didn't feel well, she would always call on her.

A lot of the time, we'd all meet at my grandparents' at Springhill Junction or at Newville Lake. So a lot of my early memories from Dad are usually connected with my grandparents. We didn't have a whole lot, and Granny and Grampy still lived in a shack. And when Dad and Mom and Granny and Grampy and me and Bernie all got together, there were a lot of us in that little shack. I remember one time, Dad had brought Bernie a record player. But there was no electricity!

When I was around six years old, Mom developed TB. And she was in the hospital for three years. At first we stayed with a friend of hers. We were sort of in foster care with her. And she wasn't the best of foster mothers. So I remember Dad came and picked us up one weekend. I remember standing there, watching the trains go by, and Dad said that we were going to go to a school and that he was going to come pick us up afterwards. So Bernie and I got on the train to go to Shubenacadie.

I remember being on the train with Bernie and he was so quiet. Bernie was never that quiet, so I knew something was going on. We got to the station and these strange people picked us up. We went up to the residential school and these strange people with black clothing brought us in. I remember walking [illegible] were gleaming. They were so

[illegible]

dormitory all by myself and it was [illegible] there waiting for my dad to come in. I was thinking, "Okay, come pick me up," because this isn't the place he told me about before we got on the train.

The next morning I woke up and Dad wasn't there. Nobody was there. So I got up and had my breakfast downstairs and just muddled around the school. Later on in the week, when the other girls started coming back to school, all of a sudden we weren't sitting at the staff table anymore. Bernie was on one side of the cafeteria and I was on the other side, and we couldn't talk to each other. So that was tough. We'd give each other hand signals just to let the other one know that we were all right.

The first while was really difficult though, because I didn't know what the rules were, I didn't know what I was supposed to do. I had a uniform. I had my play clothes. I also had never gone to a Catholic mass before. So that Catholic mass was really different. I really didn't understand.

The first year was pretty bad, because I was terrified of everything. I didn't know who these people were. I was all by myself. Bernie was on the other side, but he wasn't allowed to talk to me. We had all our meals together. And you had to eat whatever was on your plate, no ifs, ands or buts about it. If you didn't like it, that was too bad.

Every summer, we would go and stay with my grandparents. But a lot of the time, we would spend Christmas and Easter at the residential school. The first Christmas I thought I was going to go home. I told the nuns I was going home for the holidays. Christmas morning came. Everybody got up, and there was nothing for me under the tree. I thought I must be the worst person in the world. Little did I know though that my Dad had arrived the night before and there was a snowstorm. So they had put him up for the night. All of a sudden, that morning, he was there and he had fruit and candy and stuff like that. To me that was the best Christmas gift in the world. But he was so thin and drawn looking, I guess because of the alcohol. We would get letters from him, from all kinds of different places. He would write pretty regularly, at least once a month. Every now and then though, some time would go by without hearing from him, and we'd worry that something had happened to him.

After a few years at the residential school, I got used to all the rules and regulations. I was there for five years in all. And by the time I was ready to leave, I was thinking about being a nun! I was almost thirteen when I left and I was doing grade eight work. You were either sixteen or finishing grade eight when you "aged out" and got to leave. So I was thirteen, in grade seven, doing grade eight work. I figured if I could get grade eight I could get out of there real quick. By that time Bernie was already gone because he had aged out. I was there all by myself, thinking that I was never going to get out of there, that I was never going to go home. I thought I was going to be there forever. I remember the nuns talking to each other, trying to figure out what they were going to do with me, because I had almost gotten to that age.

The next thing I knew, it was October, and Dad showed up. He had never had a car before, because he had always gone from job to job. But he showed up with these people and all of a sudden, everybody was saying, "You're going to go home. You're going to go with your father."

I was allowed to pick out a coat and shoes. I guess Indian Affairs gave out vouchers for clothes. Dad took me shopping [illegible] with alcoholism for a long [illegible] fact that he loved us. And he always let us know that he loved us. I want readers to know that I was so proud of him when he quit drinking and that he had struggled so hard to stay sober. They should know how he turned his life around and started helping people. It's so nice, because now he's the dad I always thought he was. That's what I want people to know about him. That he's a very loving and beautiful person.

Mom and Dad had this very interesting relationship, all through their lives. At first they were very antagonistic towards each other. But as we got older, all of a sudden they started being friends. And then they were friends until the very end. When Mom passed, she still loved him.

Dad and I have a great relationship now. Through the years and the tribulations, as I grew into the adult I am now, Dad has always been there for me. Whenever I need him he is there. He is a wonderful grandfather and my children think he is the best thing.

My first daughter, Michelle, was like his surrogate child to him and his second wife. When I lived in Edmonton, he lived there as well. Before moving to Edmonton, I lived in Smith, Alberta. Before it was time to give birth to my second child, I was admitted to Slave Lake because I lived too far from the

ME & MY DADDY

Carol Ann and her dad, Doug

hospital. Dad would visit every night waiting for her to be born. For three nights he came, except for one, the night Nina was born. I still appreciate that memory.

They would take Michelle every weekend for a couple of months, which enabled me to take care of my infant child. It was then when Nina needed medical treatment for clubfeet. She needed to have her casts changed every two weeks. So it was a great help to have Dad there.

My grandchildren say that it is like having Santa Claus visit when he arrives for our annual Christmas dinner. It is hard to put a lifetime of memories in a few short paragraphs but I am so glad to have him as my dad.

Bernie Knockwood (left back), Carol Ann Knockwood (left front), with cousins Carson (right front) and Glendon McKnutt (right back)

Going Home

In Boston I used to read the *Micmac News*. On the back there was a whole page ad looking for alcohol and drug workers to work on the reserves. This was my dream. I said I'd love to go back and work with my people. And I'd look at that page and I'd read it and I'd read it. This friend of mine who I met at AA travelled with me a fair bit putting on meetings. He told me the truth about myself, you know. He'd know if I was full of shit and he'd tell me. He'd just let me have it. So he said, "You keep saying you want to go back and work in your field. What the hell is stopping you?" I said, "I don't have any education." "Oh, for Christ's sake," he said. "You go to prison, you go to the mental hospital. I've heard you talk over there." He said, "Bring that paper over to me. Let me read it." I brought it over to him and he read it. He said, "Where the hell does it say you have to have an education. It doesn't say anything about having an education." I said, "Well, I guess I'm nervous." My friend replied, "You know what. You go down and apply for that job. If you don't get it I'll pay your gas and expenses down and back." Not a bad deal. So I went down.

When I got to Oxford I stayed overnight with Mom and Dad and went down to Sydney the next morning early. When I got there Lawrence Paul, the chief at Membertou First Nation in Sydney, was all by himself. I walked in and said, "How ya doing Lawrence?" "Not too good," he said.

Lawrence was the one that started the group meetings. But he wasn't having too much success hiring helpers. I said, "Are you still looking for field workers?" "Yes. Are you interested?" I said, "Yeah." So he called the other two directors, and they sit down with me and they started asking me all kinds of questions. They said, "How long will it take you to move back if you are offered the position?" I said, "Yesterday." And they laughed. "Well, we don't know. We have to go back. The guys in the government have to come in, too." I finished my interview around 10:30 a.m. They got together after I left the office. When I left I drove right through, never stopped anywhere. I wanted to get back to Boston 'cause I had to go to work the next day. I'm pushing her fairly good and I come down the road — there was no Trans Canada yet, just the old highway — I'm coming down into Oxford and Mom and Dad live right on the outskirts, first house as you come in. And I seen the door open and Dad waving his hands.

And I said, "Oh god." So I stepped up a little bit and I drove in the yard and he said, "Lawrence Paul's on the phone, wants to talk to you." I said okay and I went in, took the phone, "I guess you got an ⸻ ⸻?" He said, "Yes. How soon can you come

Bernie

When Bernie came back he lazed around home for a while. He got the long hair. That's when the hippie movement was going on. And his pants, the holes in them! He went to Bob's Engineering looking for a job. I asked, "Did you dress up?" He said, "No." I told him he would never get a job that way. I said, "You get that hair cut." He had hair looked like a mane, right down to his waist. He looked at me, but he never said nothing. As I was leaving, I said, "I got a 20 dollar bill on the table. That's for a haircut. If it doesn't go for a haircut, you give it back to me when I come back," which was a week or ten days. You know Springhill, right? About halfway up that hill there used to be White's Barbershop. So I went out to visit my buddy out by the jail and I was coming back in, driving up that hill, and there I turned the corner, looked over, and guess who was going in for a haircut? Bernie. And you know what, he got all dressed up and I said, "I'll drive you." And I took him both places, Rob's engineering in Amherst and the Oxford Foundry. We went to both places on the same day, same as Bernie did the first time. But this time he was all dressed up, pants, shirt and tie. And he was hired. He got both jobs at the both places at the same time. That was a turning point for him. Four years later he went back to school. I don't know if he got his degree, I think he did, but then he went to work for the Indian organization. After he

Leaders of Mi'kmaw Lodge Treatment Centre, Eskasoni: (from left) Vincent Stevens, Wilfred Prosper, Lawrence Paul, Doug

got his education he went to work for the Confederacy. Then he went to work for the government. He was in the funding area for alcohol and drug programs. A lot of times I'd see Knockwood's name on my cheques. I said to myself, "My son signs my cheques now."

Back in the Maritimes

Lawrence and I started the counselling program in Membertou. From there we spread out slowly. He knew that we had to have more people, and I definitely agreed. We were actively looking for sober Mi'kmaw people who were willing to help us develop the program. At first we didn't have much. We had educational movies and we played the hell out of those. Other than that we only had the twelve-step program. We started our weekly sessions in Membertou. Next we went to Eskasoni and did the same thing. At first about five to seven regulars per week attended.

Lawrence hired a non-Native lady. Her name was Mary Goldman. She had a lot of years of sobriety in the program. She was very efficient and was totally fearless. Nothing that happened could shock her. From there, with Mary's initial guidance and training, we got the "pioneers": Wilfred Prosper, Ron Paul, Peter Perro and others. The goal was to put two Mi'kmaw workers on every reserve in Nova

while I was ...

Halifax, Truro and Sydney, and non-Aboriginal people hired me to do workshops because they wanted to learn how to work with our Mi'kmaw people. So I was called to do session in many places.

When I went to work in Membertou I had great difficulty re-establishing my language. I had spent years in the service, at the sanatorium and working different jobs in the non-Native world. As a result I was constantly speaking English. I never lost the hearing of Mi'kmaw words. If you talked to me in Mi'kmaq, I understood what you were saying. But I could not transfer my thoughts to Mi'kmaq and

The group attending the first session at Mi'kmaw Lodge Treatment Centre

just let it come out. I had difficulty with my own language. And it was extremely important to be able to speak with our clients in Mi'kmaq.

Lawrence had a bit of money left in the budget, so he hired me a translator. His name was Jim David Paulette, and he was absolutely flawless in his transition between English and Mi'kmaq. We spent time driving between reserves and I gained the confidence to speak Mi'kmaq again.

As we travelled across Nova Scotia working at many reserves our reputation spread. Shubenacadie reserve had always been a hold-out. The chief told us that Shubenacadie didn't need our services, as they didn't have an alcohol problem. I had actually been banned from the reserve by a former chief, Steve Knockwood, years earlier for drinking and carrying on. So I knew firsthand that there was indeed an alcohol problem. I had been a part of that problem. But as they heard about our success on other mainland reserves, Shubenacadie eventually called Lawrence Paul asking for help. John Knockwood, Steve's son, the new chief, asked for me personally to head up the program. He lifted the ban and reinstated me.

At our first meeting in Shubenacadie, people were showing up with bottles of booze tucked under their belt. They told me that they didn't need any twelve-step program. There was a house across the street from the band office. Chief John Knockwood told me that if I could clean up that house I would have passed the test.

I have always believed that the way to give people confidence and self-respect was to give them something to get sober for. The parents who lived in the house had had their children taken away. They loved their kids and wanted to have them back. I told them, "The way to get your kids back would be to get sober." So they got with the program. After they were sober for a year their children came for weekend visits. The band council was impressed and decided to fix up the house so that when the children came back they would come to a clean, sober house. After three years of sobriety the children were allowed to return home.

Vera and Eileen Marr Remember

I think to myself now that when the chief said to Doug that if he could "fix" our house, it wasn't Doug's house to fix. It was a ~~........ ...... house to fix.~~ They let it happen, by turning

At that point there was ~~only .....~~ told them all, "Be quiet, it's the chief and a social worker at the door." Dad had gone up the road and he was drinking. I went to the door and held it shut and I wouldn't let them in. Picture it, a six-year-old holding the door closed with her little foot, telling these men, "No, no, my father has just gone up the road for a minute. He should be right back."

I was trying to talk them out of coming in, and meanwhile I'm praying, "Please Dad. Please come home. They're gonna take us and you won't know where we are."

We could have easily become part of the Sixties Scoop. We have a family member who was part of that. We survived, but we were never kids either. I call it being "parentified." We always had to deal with things on an adult level.

In 1971, the eight of us kids were removed from the house. My sister and I were nine and ten years old at the time and we were the oldest. Generally, once you are taken away from your parents, the parents have one year to get the children back, otherwise their rights are relinquished and you become a permanent ward of the state. In the case of our parents, their rights weren't relinquished, because they were both working to get sober and to get us all back. And our social worker, Mrs. Robinson, and Doug stood behind that and worked with them.

Each of us eight kids were paired off and split up. My sister and I were the only two who stayed in the community. The rest were scattered in non-Native communities.

These were the days when you could just play outside all day, so while we were in care, my sister and I used to just run off and break into our parents' home, hoping that we might surprise them.

Mom and Dad struggled with getting sober. They really tried. The turning point, to me, was that Dad had to be back for a court date. He was down in Maine, harvesting blueberries or potatoes, and he had to be back in court or we'd be adopted out. Our father hiked back from Maine and met the date. After that, our social worker, Mrs. Robinson, told us we'd be going home soon. She didn't know the exact date, but our parents were getting sober.

I remember the day that we first started being able to go home for visits with our parents. It was November 17, 1972. At first those visits were hard, because it was tough to leave. You'd always hope that this visit was the one where you got to stay with Mom and Dad, not just for a few hours at a time.

That's where we met Doug. We were only nine and ten at the time, but even at that age we knew what he stood for. We knew the security that you felt when Doug was there. He's been our friend ever since. Our second father. Our guardian angel.

Dad would have his rough patches. He'd get so frustrated and angry sometimes, but he never drank again. He stuck to his word. I remember when our youngest sister had cancer. She was in the hospital in Halifax and Mom and Dad were supposed to go visit her that day. Dad was sleeping on the couch and Mom woke him up. He just jumped up and exploded and punched this birdcage we had. The bird went flying, but it was all right. Mom just got us out of the house and told us to "go get Doug." Once Doug came we knew it was going to be okay.

When Doug talks about handing out educational materials in the community, I remember that. Dad had a box of these old cassette tapes that he would play when he couldn't make it .... I remember sitting there with those

We weren't afraid then, because ...

role that Doug played for us, Dad was playing for them. After that, even though they called our house a "flunky" house, our home had boundaries. And Mom and Dad set those boundaries. All of Dad's so-called buddies respected that too. Because you wouldn't mess with my Dad once he said, "Don't do this."

When I look back, I see that we were the norm, part of that statistic. And with a lot of people growing up, our age, that cycle continues on to this day. What made us so different? How did we not end up like that? I remember making those promises, at an early age, that my kids wouldn't go through this. They won't see us falling down drunk, or getting beaten up.

That's why Doug will always be our angel. He will always be our constant, because at the time he came into our lives, people didn't believe there would be something better. We were too busy surviving. And really, I always thought I'd be too busy fighting. And Doug told us, "It's not always going to be like this. We can fight but it will always be in a good way."

If Doug wasn't there, there would be a big chapter in our lives that would be gone. Lord knows how we would have ended up. Our dad was a strong man, but even strong men need help. I think the most important part was that we knew Doug was coming to visit Dad. There was someone who would come by to take care of Dad, because he had to be taken care of. He took care of us eight kids and his wife. Doug was always his constant. Everybody should have one constant in their life. If they can have two, that would be great. Ours would be Doug.

Theresa Meuse Remembers

I have known Elder Doug my whole life. He was a close friend of my parents, and he and his family visited often.

When I was a pre-teenager, Elder Doug and Lawrence Paul from Membertou brought the AA twelve-step program to the community of Bear River. This program was a new provincial initiative to teach our people about the negative effects of alcohol and help others learn to refrain from alcohol use. There was also programming known as Al-Anon — to help those living with someone who abuses alcohol have better coping mechanisms, and Alateen — the same approach designed for teenagers.

When I was 13, Doug became the sponsor of our Alateen group. And, like any good Elder, he spent his time helping us understand alcoholism and taught us coping methods so we could have a better relationship with the person in our family that used alcohol.

There were about ten of us in the group and we met at the local church on a regular basis. Doug would always start us off in prayer and conduct informal meetings that lasted about an hour or so. Even though we sat in pews, in a way Doug exposed us to our first talking circles. Each one of us was given a chance to talk and share what was on our minds even if it was something troubling us.

Doug had a wonderful ability for keeping us calm when the topics were not so pleasant. Just his gentle demeanour and the way he smiled assured us we were safe and could trust each other in our talks. Doug would have pamphlets and information for us along with of course goodies and treats. We even got to do craftwork and artwork as a way of expressing ourselves and having a positive attitude.

. . . . taking place for about a year or so

. . . . same to me.

So, we got to travel to Sydney, Cape Breton, and stayed at a hotel and I shared my room with a friend. During the day Doug and other adults would gather us in plenary sessions and workshops. Overall it was all so exciting and since then, Elder Doug has been one of my favourite people.

I can remember thinking at the time, "Why can't everybody just be like Doug?" He was a kind, gentle man and forty years later, in my heart, he hasn't changed a bit.

Throughout my adult years, we continued to work together on many projects and his family stayed in touch with our family. Doug remains a person in my life equal to a family member. Despite all the hardship and sorrow Doug experienced throughout this life, his outlook on life and smile on his face remain.

Elder Doug is truly one of a kind. A very respectful member of our people and his spirit provides nothing but positive energy. I am so thankful to be able to contribute to his memoir and hope others will get the chance to meet Doug and feel the instant love connection he shares with everyone. *Wela'lin* Elder Doug.

Growing the Program

The program was having great success. There were twelve-step programs in every reserve in Nova Scotia. There were also active education programs to explain to people the dangers of alcohol. By this time Lawrence and I were household names in many communities.

But we both thought that we needed further training to increase our counselling skills, so we attended further education courses. In 1972, I attended a summer school at Rutgers University in New Jersey, and Lawrence went to summer course at Carleton University. In 1973, I attended a summer course at George Brown College in Toronto. These programs were helpful but I wanted to get more training in professional counselling. I wanted to go and learn to be a counsellor, and to come back and train our guys and gals. Lawrence and I agreed that I should go. He said, "Doug you got everything rolling so well even I can handle it." There was a two-year counselling program at George Brown College. I applied and was accepted. So I was off to George Brown College.

Volunteering

When I was in Toronto I used to put on meetings. A lot of times these meetings were difficult. I went into one place outside of Toronto. This was after I was sober for years and I was going around looking for courses and I got to know this chap who was this liaison man for the city of Toronto and the prison outside of Toronto, going north. There was a prison there where they put about 600 prisoners and they used to have a meeting on Sunday afternoons. They took volunteers from Toronto. I knew one of the guys and he said, "They get kinda rowdy out here now and again." I said, "That's okay. I go to Walpole. They get rowdy down there, too." So I went in and the older man was ahead of me and I watched the actions that were going on. There were close to 400 of them. I'm looking at paper flying through the air, cigarettes flying through the air. They was throwing them at one another. I was watching this and the old fellow was still carrying on, so when it came my turn to speak, I said, "Gentlemen, I'm sorry, we're going to have a little break. You have a cigarette break, do it now. You need a drink of water or drink of coffee, do it now. I'll give you five minutes to do all ——————," I said, "look outside. See how beautiful it is out there.

you guys if you want to exchange—g
to do, I want you to do that now. I'll give you five minutes to do what you have to do. If you have to go to the bathroom. I'm only going to speak for twenty minutes, twenty-five minutes." They all done what they had to do, smokes and so on. I got up and I gave forth my little presentation and when I finished I got a standing ovation. One said, "You know, for us in here trying to learn something, it's very difficult when the guys are throwing cigarettes and making noise. We need more people like you to tell us to sit down, shut up and listen. You done that well today." They all listened and that gave me a little more strength to do these things.

I did not complete the course because during my second year at George Brown I was asked to come to deal with difficulties at Manitou College. Manitou College was located on the vacated Bomarc missile site in La Macaza, Quebec, north of Montreal in the Laurentian Mountains.

New Career at Manitou College
The Mohawk and Mi'kmaw students were at loggerheads. The kids used to get a "payday" from their reserves, and a couple of the Mohawk and Mi'kmaw students had gotten drunk at the pub and almost raised a riot. The next day, the director general, George Miller, was up for putting these two students out. But all the Mohawk students and all

the Mi'kmaw students were down there supporting these two, lined up in the gymnasium. And none of them would budge. George sat with them all afternoon and he couldn't get these students to move. Bernie called me that night and explained the situation. I said, "I guess I'll take the rest of the week off. I'll be down by ten o'clock."

Well, when I arrived it was just as it was explained. The Mi'kmaw kids were on this side, the Mohawks on that side. George was trying to convince them that the two instigators should go, and that the rest of the students would continue their education. It wasn't working, so finally he asked if I would talk to them. As I walked out on the stage, I saw three of the little guys that were in the teenagers programming group from Eskasoni. When I walked out they all looked at me and smiled.

I stood there looking at them for a couple minutes, then I said, "It's a shame that you're all going home when you have the opportunity to make a new life for yourselves with more education. You have nice places to live. There are three-bedroom homes here, with kitchens and dining rooms. They're beautiful. So what are you doing?" I said, "You don't want to budge. So you're going to support a couple of people that may have an alcohol problem. They caused you guys to get mad and fight last night. You're just starting at this beautiful college that will move you forward and get you going somewhere that you want to be in life. Then here's two little drunks and if they stay, they'll have another fight and somebody's gonna get hurt. So why are you backing them up, throwing your own chances away? You gotta start looking after yourselves and look out for your futures." I told them, "If I were you, I'd be helping those guys on the bus."

Those little guys from Eskasoni looked at me and one of them said, "You're right Mr. Knockwood, we're going to help our guy on the bus home tonight." The Mohawks decided that they'd help see their guy off too. And in that way the school year continued for everybody else.

The board of directors saw what I had done in terms of helping to quell the crisis. The next day they invited me over for dinner. Bernie had temporarily excused himself from the board. They approached me and asked if I would consider staying on as Manitou College's guidance counsellor. I wound up staying there for about a week, get-thing settled again. My instructor at George Brown wanted

there was a greater chance for

women getting their education, while the young men were back home. So the jealousy part was sometimes there. There was a fair amount of drinking at the pub, but they weren't involved in any great trouble like that first time when they refused to leave the campus. I had a couple of sessions with the students after that and things seemed to settle down. There were no more fights at the pub, that's for sure.

I got very interested in the education aspect of what was going on there. Because the educational model at Manitou wasn't the same as the Western model, or the residential school setting, where you have to do this and this and this, and if you don't follow along, then you get marked back. At Manitou, we were able to help guys and gals who were having difficulty in making their marks. George Miller and the staff were able to help those that were academically not strong enough to work through it. The professors realized the importance of helping Aboriginal students. They spent far more time with the students than they would in a regular university setting. You go into a university, the professor tells you do something in twenty minutes, then you pass in the paper. Your marks are either good, bad or indifferent. Here, if professors saw a student struggling, they'd actually help them bring their marks back up.

The College was set up as an education centre for Native people. After the crisis was resolved things were rolling wonderfully. When they gave me the position of counsellor and recruiter, it was a boost to my ego and income. What happened was, in the spring and summer when all the students went home, I went recruiting to different reserves asking them if they wanted someone to come in and explain the program. They made me director of that program. So I travelled all over eastern Canada going to places that had applied for information. That's what I did in the summer, then back to school in the fall. The next summer I did the same thing.

There were a few places that were difficult, for example among the Montagnais because I didn't speak French. I came into Restigouche, where one of the band member's wives decided to go to Manitou College, not to go to school but to live with a young man to train him how to be at home with a woman. When the chief introduced me, I gave a little spiel about my duties, and he's sitting in the back, listening. I had a few jokes in between. The woman's husband said, "Manitou College." You could hear a pin drop, 'cause he knew that his wife left for Manitou. "I wouldn't send my dog to Manitou College." And everybody gasped. I waited till it had settled down a little bit and I said, "You know I have many people in Manitou College — some great people — future leaders. But if I had someone come to Manitou College with the attitude that you have, we would probably kick his ass out of there." And everybody laughed. And he never said any more after that. He let me do my presentation. When they came and wished me well and talked about it, he didn't come over and acknowledge me. But that was okay because I had the majority of the band council backing me up and that was a nice feeling.

It was at Manitou College that I met Kathy. Kathy was working for Indian Affairs in Northern Quebec. In the summertime, when my students went on holiday, they opened up the college for other Aboriginal educational purposes. Kathy was the assistant for the James Bay area, which covered quite a distance. She brought her students down to Manitou in the summer. I was out recruiting in Ontario and part of Quebec. I used to come back to the college — in the summer months I was probably there four or five times. One day the superintendent said to me, "Where are you from?" I said, "Nova Scotia." "Oh you're an Easterner." "Yeah." "I have an Easterner working for me. She b̲r̲i̲n̲g̲s̲ the students out here from James Bay. She's here now. You'll

more! So we went out and

and I'll never forget the look they gave me. Kathy had everything set up. But her friend had a fourteen-year-old cousin or something. Kathy had everything lined up and the centre seat was hers and the little fourteen-year-old took it. I wish you could have seen the look on her face 'cause that's where Kathy would have sat. That's where Kathy was setting up for. And this fourteen-year-old jumps in her seat. So Kathy had to sit behind me. She wasn't too pleased. When she was setting up for the band and the barbeque and everything, she said to me, "That little bitch is not sitting in that seat going home." I think that's where the relationship came together. I met her a couple of times after that and then I went away recruiting again. When I got back she was still there. So we went out together for two weeks or so. The last time I came back they were getting ready to go out to James Bay. She said, "What do you do besides working here?" "I do alcohol and drug education. I go to prisons and things like that." She asked, "Do you work with school kids, school children?" "No, never did," I responded. She said, "No different, they sit and listen to you. It would be nice if you come up and do a couple of weeks' workshop." "Yeah," I said. "It really would be nice."

Kathy spoke to her supervisor, and her supervisor allowed her to bring me up. She got me up there for two weeks. I stayed with her and that's when the relationship blossomed. When her school term was up the next summer and she said, "I'm resigning." I asked, "Where are you going?" She said, "I don't know yet. I might go back to New Brunswick." That was her home. Then she said, "I thought about Ontario." Manitou College had to close because their funding was cut off.

Bernie Remembers

At the time that Manitou College got started, I was in Montreal going to university at Sir George Williams. It was among the universities in Quebec that had joined up with the Native North American Studies Institute, which was an organization formed to help First Nations people at that time to get their higher education. George Williams University offered some courses in Native studies and Native literature and other things that were used to promote Native awareness.

I was extremely intrigued by the Native-specific content of some of the courses I was taking at Sir George. When I found out there would be more of the same at Manitou College, I arranged to transfer there in '73. What it was for me was an awakening and an awareness of who and what I was. Up until that point in time I was a lost person, coming out of a residential school, working in the non-Native workforce as a redneck welder.

How my dad got involved at Manitou College is that there was a slight disagreement between some of the Mi'kmaw and Mohawk students, which involved some alcohol. And it risked spilling over. The upshot of the whole thing is that the administration needed to have a counsellor come in and talk to the students. We needed someone who was knowledgeable of alcohol and drugs and knew First Nations people. To me, that sounded like my dad. He was up in Toronto, studying at George Brown College. I called him up and I said, "You have to come up here and help us out."

We had CEGEP courses, which is the post–high school

program for Quebec. We got our French programming accreditation as a college through Ahuntsic College, and Dawson College in Montreal provided the English ... accreditation. All courses were directed towards

Cree, Montagnais, Inuit, Mohawk, was dynamic, new, challenging, supportive, extremely exciting and I wouldn't have missed it for the world.

Because we were such a diverse group that came together in one place, we had our arguments, squabbles. One of the things we found that didn't work was the concept of a student council that you might find in any other educational institution. Normally, you'd have a president, a vice-president, a secretary, a treasurer, and on and on. At Manitou, there were too many diverse groups, with too much national pride, to make that model work. "Who are you to tell me what to do?" Students would say. "What gives you the right to come into my territory and tell me how to govern?"

Everything was at an impasse. Our student council was bickering. Nothing was getting done. And the school administration was getting frustrated. I remember everyone was sitting around, and the Mohawk students were saying, "This wouldn't have happened if we had arranged this like our grand council." So the rest of the student council said, "Okay, we'll take you up on your grand council. How does it work?"

So we listened and set ourselves up as a grand council. The Mi'kmaw students were to have a representative. The Mohawk students were to have a representative. Everyone was to get a representative. And we all came together as a council.

The next step was to decide who was going to take the students' message to the administration. We needed one representative to take all of our concerns. And the role of this spokesperson would be to take our message forward, which was arrived at on a consensus basis. The spokesperson would not have the authority to change what we had said in council.

Then, the spokesperson would return with the position of the administration, who would either agree or disagree with what we had put forward. They'd just bring the message back and say what had been said. Then we'd go talk to the rest of the student body, and things would go back and forth in this manner.

I got appointed as the person to take our messages to the administration. I was the spokesman for the grand council. The first couple of meetings were interesting, to say the least. The administration was so used to having an answer right then and there. But I would just tell them, "I can't agree to anything. I have to take it back to the grand council and discuss it. So either you put that behind you or we don't do it at all. We're at an impasse."

After a while it turned into a really good process. Students felt that their voices did matter in the administration and in the running of the place. It provided a lot of open debate on a lot of sensitive issues going on in the college.

One of them was the inclusion of Inuit students as part of the process. At that time they weren't considered "Indians." We said there's no difference between them and someone living in a lower part of Canada. The only difference is that they are living in a land of ice and snow. But they had lot of issues related to colonial contact and not being listened to.

One of the other things that I found was unique was that there were a lot of arts programs at Manitou College: sculpture, painting, carving and other things. The teachers encouraged the

First Nations students to come at art from their perspectives, rather than saying, "this is how it should be done" or anything like that. The teachers didn't impose a value system. They just ⋯⋯ the students were doing and provided direction

the front of the carving on ⋯⋯ I asked. He just explained, "I looked at the wood and I saw a mother bear and two cubs looking at me and I just took away everything that didn't look like that." The artistic talent that some students had! And it wasn't being appreciated.

Dad came along and started working with the students. He resolved a lot of problems related to alcohol and drugs. Having someone that the students could sit with and talk to, that they didn't have to spend three-quarters of their time explaining who they were and where they came from, was incredibly important. Instead they had someone who was already there with them. Someone who had already been there, done that and lost the t-shirt!

When Dad was there, his role in the whole thing was also one of inter-tribal mediation. Because there was always a bone of contention between the Mohawks and the Mi'kmaq and the Cree and the Montagnais, for example. If Dad hadn't been there, it would have self-destructed. Because the students needed someone who understood and who could talk to them, and gain their respect and trust. And in the end, they all respected and trusted him. It took a while, maybe eight months, but that was a lot shorter time than it would have taken for anybody else.

By the time the school year ended, they had his trust and

they were glad that he was coming back to continue discussing the things they had discussed. It also helped to know that he was there if they needed help on settling in when they came back.

Dianne Spencer Remembers

I was working in Northern Quebec, in Fort George, which is now the Cree Nation of Chisasibi. Kathy came in there to teach when I had just finished my first year. I believe this was 1965. I left and went off to college, but then came back. So, we both did our second years at the school together and then we were together for four years after that. We shared an apartment and Kathy was definitely my best friend.

We had a great time in the North. The administration encouraged us to not associate with the Cree village, but Kathy and I did just the opposite. We would sneak out late at night and go to the village dances. They would start at midnight and wouldn't end until the sun came up in the morning. We had sewing bees with the local women. We had cooking bees. We kept busy with whatever we could do in the village.

There were probably four or five hundred Cree living there at the time. There was no power in the village back then, so everybody just used lanterns. There were lots of dog teams. Everybody heated their homes with wood stoves. And they were all very friendly and open to meeting new people.

Kathy did a lot — she and the two other teachers — to encourage the kids to speak their own language. We were all trying to learn Cree. Kathy and the kids ended up taking the old *Dick and Jane* readers and translating them into Cree and using that for their schooling. It was a very different scenario than the stories we hear now about residential schools.

These days, they talk about the abuse that went on in residential schools. In our generation, nobody spoke about any of that. It was all so hush-hush. But I remember one of the senior boys came forward to me and told me that the principal was abusing some of the boys. I told Kathy. She said, "I can't let

House in Toronto in two

to someone who would take action.

That spring, they transferred the principal and his wife out of Fort George. They didn't fire him, they just transferred him out to Old Crow, a day school in the Yukon. He knew his transfer was based on our letter, and he was very angry.

The administration out of Quebec City was very aware of Kathy's abilities. If she found anything wrong with the curriculum, anywhere, they'd hear about it. I remember one time the administrators had come to Fort George on a visit. Kathy went up to the head administrator and told him, "How am I going to read to these kids about a cow? If you want me to teach this, then bring me in a cow so they can at least see what it looks like." She liked to push the buttons and find the limits, but always to the kids' benefit.

The school in Fort George only went to grade eight, so the administration started shipping the kids down south to the high schools in the Rouyn-Noranda area and to Val-d'Or. When they first went down, some of the parents who were boarding these kids weren't prepared for another culture. They didn't know how to handle it. So a bunch of us teachers and administrators flew down and met with the boarding parents so that they could see the interaction with these students and realize that the differences in culture weren't anything negative — that people were people and to just embrace it.

Kathy became the curriculum director working with Indian and Northern Affairs, out of Val-d'Or, at which point we lost touch for a few years. She was the exact person for the job, and she worked her butt off to get it. I stayed teaching for a few more years, but one summer I went on a holiday with a stop at Manitou College. Doug wasn't there at the time, but Kathy told me that she'd met a fellow there and that he was really nice. She told me that one evening she was leaving the campus store, and it was raining really hard. All of the sudden this guy came out of the store and jumped in the back of her car, and it was Doug! He asked her for a drive home. So that's how they met. Conveniently it was raining, so at least he had an excuse!

The thing was, I knew Doug from when I was a kid because he used to drink with my father! They were certainly a good team together. They were both very active in the twelve-step programming. Kathy embraced that all very easily. I would say that they were meant for each other. It was guaranteed that wherever she went, she gave her all and left her mark.

Yellowknife

At this time I saw an advertisement for a job in Yellowknife. It seemed like a new and interesting opportunity. At the time I was still seeing Patsy, who was working for the Ontario Addictions Foundation. She had a good job up there. She was all set to quit her job and come north with me. That was before Kathy stuck her nose in. So I said to Kathy, "I'm going to Yellowknife. There is a new job there." I said, "They have a school system up there. Maybe you can get a job?" So Kathy wound up coming with me. We started our life together then. It was nice. We went to Yellowknife at our own expense not knowing whether we had a job or not. I bought a new Fury, Plymouth Fury. We travelled in comfort. Everything was sailing along.

When we got to Saskatchewan, the frigging transmission let go. They had to send to the States for a replacement. Oh god, I thought, it is going to take forever. Then she said, "I'll phone Dad." Dad was a big insurance ~~~ in New Brunswick. So in no time at all we had a thousand bucks.

also on the board. ~~~~

It turned out that the Yellowknife school board was looking for an education counsellor. We arrived just as they were running an ad. Kathy applied and they didn't hesitate. They hired her right away.

When we arrived in Yellowknife we didn't have a place to sleep. We slept in the car. I thought, holy shit, what'll we do this winter. Anyways, the superintendent of education came and said to Kathy, "There's an apartment being vacated today." It had two or three bedrooms. Anyway, it was a nice one. It was teachers quarters. So that's where we moved to. We stayed at that apartment I guess probably three years, and then there was a trailer for sale. Trailers were going because miners were coming and going. We got a 27-footer for $11,000. Later we bought a trailer up in Franklin Park. They were nice trailers up there and this fellow was moving out and he sold it to us for $22,000. We stayed there for the rest of our time in Yellowknife.

When I arrived in Yellowknife, all they had was a simple, five-bed detoxification centre. At the time there was an executive director, a secretary and three nurses who had come from Edmonton. The secretary was a recovered alcoholic with ten years' sobriety, so she knew about recovery. The nurses had never worked in a detox program before. The executive director didn't have much training about how to run a detox centre, so the secretary was carrying the ball. The detox centre had been running for about a year and a half when I arrived. But it was not doing its job. It had largely become a flophouse for miners returning to the North. The miners would come to Yellowknife for a few weeks to blow their money. When they were in Yellowknife they used the detox centre as a place to crash for free and dry out before they went back to work again. The next time they came back they would do it all over again. There was supposed to be a five-day limit on staying at the centre, but these miners would stay ten days or two weeks waiting to go back to their jobs. At first, because I was new, I didn't say anything. Then one night while I was driving home, I noticed one of the Indian guys, his name was Lawrence, leaning up against a post. He had been drinking and was in no shape to stay outside. I pulled up and said to him, "Lawrence, what the hell are you doing out here? You need to get home." But he told me that his family had gone to Edmonton and nobody had left him a key. I said, "Get in and I'll take you to the detox." "They won't take me there. They don't take Indians there." I said, "You come with me and we will get this sorted out."

When we arrived at the centre there was one bed available. I told the nurse on duty to get things ready for Lawrence. The nurse said, "I can't do that." I said to her, "I am the new detox rehab counsellor and this man needs help."

She told me that the bed was reserved for a man arriving on a flight from Edmonton. "Tough," I said. "Give this man the bed." It was then that I started to look around. I went to a fella in a bed and asked him, "How long have you been here?" "Two weeks," he told me. I told him to be gone in the morning. Another fella had been there ten days and another two weeks. So I put the run to them all.

I called a staff meeting. I said to the nurses, "Ladies, when it comes to issues of health and hospitalization you got more education and training than I do. But when it comes to alcoholism you have to take a new approach. When an alcoholic needs help, they need it now. This is not a hotel. You can't be reserving beds for somebody coming in the next night. If I hadn't taken Lawrence here and insisted that he stay, he would have been outside all night."

Coming home from the land — Doug, Kathy, Bert and Maeanne,
North West Territories

Another incident involved a young man who had killed two RCMP officers. I knew the story. His mother was a shaman. She believed that the RCMP were a threat to the community. It was her who had gotten her son to kill the Mounties. I knew that he had killed the officers at his mother's request and out of what he thought was his duty. He needed help, and I wanted to admit him to the detox centre. When I told the staff that I was bringing him in they told me that they would all quit if I admitted that murderer. I thanked them for letting me know because it would give me time to find new staff. In the end they did not quit.

Once the people who came for counselling and the drunks got sober enough, I got the counsellors to push as much AA as I possibly could without going over the line and then encourage them to go to the meetings that were being held. In the beginning we were short of trained staff. There were three nurses who worked as counsellors but I couldn't get them to go to any alcohol and drug meetings. I went there as an alcohol consultant, I guess. The director didn't have any knowledge of the programs — AA, Al-Anon or anything. He got the job because he had mental health training. He was the one who started the program. Because his secretary was a member of AA, I had an ally in the system already. She knew what I was doing when I got after the nurses. She would tell the boss, "Doug did this today." So when they went and complained to him I already knew what was going on. They wondered how the hell it happened. But my ally was good. She fed me what was going on. Before I came, sometimes it would take the guys who stayed there anywhere from ten days to thirty days. They were the guys that made all that money up North. And that's where they came to get dried out.

Slowly things began to take shape. The five-bed unit began to do what it was supposed to do, provide a five-day place for people to get sober. After demonstrating how effective a properly run detox centre could be, we were able to persuade our funders to provide the funds so we could expand and start a halfway house. We got some funding from government sources but most of our funding came from private and community donations.

The Giant Coal Mine donated two of their trailers. Each of them had ten beds, which became our twenty-bed halfway house. We had people coming to the halfway house from all over the North. Many of our clients were ex-inmates on parole. Some came to get treatment and finish their sentence. We had success with getting quite a few guys sober but many of them screwed up with us and went back to prison. We did not have twelve-step meetings at the halfway house. But there were meetings in Yellowknife two nights a week and people at the house would go to those meetings.

When we first went to Yellowknife I did all my work in the city with the detox centre and the halfway house. I got into sports. I was a bowler. We went to the Dominion Finals in Winnipeg. I was a member of that. And curling. I curled a bit. The reason I did that was I had to have something for my clients. There was no recreation for them in that centre. So I had to do this in order to bring them out to exercise. So I had to do that as well. And that's how we got the program. But it was good for me too because it gave me an education on the other people a bit.

up a new program and they

up. So we had supper together and Kathy came with us and he sat there and outlined the job. Man, I could see her excitement. The job was so good I decided to give it a whirl. If they hire me, okay. If they don't hire me I have nothing to lose.

I was happy and well established in Yellowknife but Kathy said that she would love to go. So I flew down to Edmonton. I passed the interview with flying colours. I was hired to work with the director of the program. They had an awful backlog of alcoholics coming in there and nobody to work with them. They had professionals there — doctors, social workers — but no alcohol workers. They didn't know how. They were dealing with Aboriginal people all over Alberta but they never had anyone who could identify with these guys and gals.

The job was good pay, a good position. Government job. Most money I ever made as a professional. I was so happy. My job was to assist the directors of the Workers' Compensation Board with addiction problems with board clients. The medical staff at the compensation board were all doctors but they had little experience or knowledge dealing with addiction recovery. In addition, they did not have the skills to deal with the Aboriginal clients. That's why they hired me. On the job I travelled a lot. I worked with another fellow and we visited clients from across the province. He and I set up treatment programs for the compensation board around the province. We set up the entire program in three years.

Kathy had a job with the Alberta Indian Education Commission. She wrote a proposal, beautiful. I always kick my ass or kick hers for not keeping a duplicate copy because the crazy superintendent tore it up.

We were socialites. We had these prestige jobs and we used to go to the parties. Anywhere there was a session going on, professional people, we were always invited. It helped us to grow together too. It helped us with our marriage, in our relationship. Her and I never fought. This evening Kathy said, "I don't want to drink tonight." I said, "Okay." So I got a big bottle of pop, put it in the fridge with everyone else's. We had our lunch, took our Coke with us and we drank. Then we went out on the other floor, didn't know what we were going to do, but at the end of it we had sort of a time for an hour. We had music and when we went home we left a half a bottle of Coke there. The next day, Kathy said, "You know, we fooled everyone last night. They thought we were both drinking. A girl came to Kathy and said, 'My god, your husband sure knows how to handle his drink.'"

I came home one night and Kathy said, "There's a phone call for you." "What for?" She said, "Did you apply for a job in the Yukon?" I said, "No." They had called and said my interview was on Saturday morning. I said. "Oh. That's the expensive one." "Yeah, 55 thousand to start." What happened was that I had met this guy from Winnipeg. Him and I were on a workshop in Lethbridge and he got to be a good friend of mine. He told me about a job in Whitehorse. The guy from Winnipeg said, "Are you applying for that job in Whitehorse?" I decided to give it a shot. The plane used to leave Monday, Wednesday and Friday. Then it came back Tuesday, Thursday and Saturday. Anyways, we went down, we went down together, and we had fun. Had a big dinner when we got down there, talked about old times and all that.

The next day I had to go for an interview. At the end of the interview, the director said, "What would you say your equivalency was to your life, work and education that you have. What would you say your level

Doug's mom, Ann Mary, and dad, Freeman Bernard, celebrating their sixtieth anniversary in Yellowknife

of education would be?" I said, "Grade ten." "Okay." About twenty minutes later his secretary came over. She talked to me probably about fifteen or twenty minutes and said, "Mr. Knockwood, what would you say was your education standard?" She made me say grade eleven or twelve. The superintendent, who was doing all the interviews, the secretary and the director, the three of them came to me and wanted to change my level of education to grade twelve. They said I had the level of grade twelve. But I didn't know that.

So my friend said, "Are you going to take the job?" I said, "No, I wanted to but my wife thinks it's too soon." She said, "If you take the job I'm going back home."

Back to Yellowknife

We had been in Edmonton three years. I trained the friggin doctors. When we were finished setting up the program the compensation board directors said, "Thank you very much. We can look after it from here."

So Kathy and I went back up to the territories. I was hired by the government to set up alcohol education programs in some fifteen communities in the Eastern Arctic Region. I travelled with a magistrate in the Northwest Territories because there was no sense in hiring a plane for just one person. We went out to the community. I would go and do some work with the people. I would probably only see one or two people, but it was one or two people I wouldn't have seen otherwise. And that's how we built the program. The winter was almost impossible but when I got them going I managed to keep them together. I was able to bring them from their community to a bigger community to have a workshop. I had three communities come in together. They would support one another. That's how we built the program.

The programs were set up specifically for Inuit people. Once the program was set up in each community, it was put under a community program director. The community directors answered to me. I was the overseer of all the programs. Back in Yellowknife, Kathy taught while I was setting up the program.

Bert, our first son, was born when Kathy and I were back to the territories. We almost lost him because he was premature. During the birth there was a lack of oxygen and his blood was bad. The doctors had to drain his blood completely. It was pretty shaky for a while and he could have died if we didn't find the right type of blood donor. The doctors in Yellowknife thought they might have to fly him out to Edmonton. They put a call out through the hospital staff to see if anyone was a donor match and thankfully one of the x-ray technicians was identical. That's how Bert survived. But that was certainly a scare, so we figured that was all the children we were going to have.

Kathy though had always wanted a girl. I told her that would suit me fine. So we put out to adopt a little girl. Then lo and behold, one morning she woke up and her period didn't start. That tells you something. So Kathy was pregnant again.

At the same time, the call came in that our girl was ready for adoption. I was in Frobisher Bay (Iqaluit) doing a workshop and Kathy called me and said, "Are you going to be able to come home this weekend?" I told her I certainly hoped so. So Kathy asked me if I'd mind heading in to Inuvik to pick up our girl, who was coming in from ~~...~~ I told her of course, that I was ready to head out.

a little girl. "They must have forgot~~...~~ she'll be here."

The next thing I knew the nurse walked into the airport lounge holding this little bundle. "Mrs. Knockwood?" she said. "Here's your little girl." And she handed the bundle to Kathy. I said, "Holy so and so and so and so!" "I told you it was a little girl," said Kathy. "I didn't say how big she was." So we got our angel. She changed everything and it was beautiful. She came into our world, a little bundle just this big, with sharp black eyes and no sign of a smile. Just a stern, hearty look, when she looked at a toy. She became captain of the household.

Then Glen arrived. It completed the home. As the boys grew, they accepted her and looked after her like she was a piece of gold. They looked after each other, loved each other, and they loved their mom and dad.

Back to Nova Scotia

After three years we decided we wanted to go back to the Maritimes. We went back to New Brunswick and stayed there for two months. We didn't know what we were going to do but we knew we had to move back to Nova Scotia. My band number was in Nova Scotia. That's when you were allowed to have band numbers. Kathy, by virtue of being my wife, had a band number as well.

Kathy, Doug, Maeanne and Bert, Yellowknife

So we came back and we went to Sheubenacadie. At the time Joe Denny was the executive director of the rehabilitation program in Eskasoni. He had succeeded Lawrence Paul. I had met him a few times before I left. The program at Eskasoni was already going full blast. Joe had taken over his father-in-law's position when he died. He'd just retired but still had his nose in the business. I came back and he called up. He called Shubenacadie and asked, "What's Doug doing?" They said, "Nothing." Joe said, "Tell him to come and see me." I said to Kathy, "We have a whole truckload of furniture. What are we going to do with it?" The school board had offered Kathy a position. So I said, "It looks good. You know, we take the basic salary, that's good enough for us." We had a fair amount of money in the bank and a big truckload of furniture. We were ready to go to Eskasoni. A guy offered to rent us a house at a nice spot on the reserve. We were all loaded and ready to go and he called me and said, "It's all set Doug. Come down and move in. Everything's ready to go." We drove into the yard and the guy who promised to rent us the house said, "I changed my mind." So here I am with a big truckload of furniture and a carload of kids. He was never my friend after that.

We drove to Sydney. Stayed in a hotel for a week or so. The kids had room to move around and go to the pool and we had our orien-

Money's no problem. ....

as well." Again I said, "Okay." When I went home that night I said, "You're looking at an alcohol and drug consultant." "What?" said Kathy. I said, "I got to build a treatment centre." Kathy said, "Oh my god. What next!"

It didn't take Joe long to get things going. As soon as I said yes, he had the carpenters out building the centre. The centre was a fifteen-bed unit. I trained the staff. I had them sent out to different places to get experience, then brought them back and put them in the program. But everyone smoked in those days and I only had the one lung. I couldn't see them when I was teaching because of the smoke.

My one lung was catching me up. I started to get tired and weak. It was too much for me. I wanted to resign. They didn't want me to go but I said, "I can't hack it, too much smoke." I used to see a Doctor White. He told me a year before, "Get out of there, Doug. You're going to shorten your lifespan. Get out of there. I can get you a pension. You know that." So I came out, and they gave me a pension. So we came back to Shubenacadie.

When we came back we lived up on the hill in a broken-down old place. The counsellors told me there were new contracts for a new building and that I was on the list. I said, "I'm gonna get this one." The house was brand new. They built it right for me.

Then I got involved in building the treatment centre in

Shubenacadie. The centre had only seven beds and there was smoking downstairs. They were not allowed to smoke upstairs. I got the program going and I said, "I can't do any more. Get somebody else." I had had just enough. I go to sleep at night, it's alcohol and drugs. I wake up in the morning, it's alcohol and drugs. My wife's lying there with arms open, nobody getting in between. So I retire. I was close to seventy.

Theresa Morris Remembers

I've known Doug all of my life. He's a very good friend of my mom and my dad. When I started working here at the Eagle's Nest, Doug was coming in and talking with the clients here, the residents. He would come in and he would tell his story about his time with addictions and the work that he did. The clients really took to him 'cause he was so humble, he was so real. I would say that he not only inspired myself but people he encountered, the residents here. He would do AA meetings and then he would do the one-on-ones. I would call him a cultural therapist. He was quite inspirational, motivating people for change. That's the way I see Doug. He's an agent of change. Although he has said change is hard, it's not impossible and good change is right around the corner. He used to say that. I think he inspired me in that way.

You can't really assume that just because somebody is First Nations that they know their history, that they know their culture, because they don't. A lot of times they do not. And a lot of times clients that come through these doors are learning it for the first time. Because all of our programs here at the Eagle's Nest are culturally based. Everything is culturally based surrounding addictions. So Doug really enhanced that. He would put pride and dignity where there was none before. He would talk about the history and how strong our ancestors are, and I remember him saying one time, and I still use this today. He would say,

"The blood of our ancestors is flowing in your veins. That same blood is in your veins. And look what they endured! Look what they survived! And we're still here today."

~~~ ~~~ould tell his story and it would be very real and it

especially for graduations. ~~ ~~ open and close and he'll do it in English and then he'll speak Mi'kmaq. He keeps it very positive. He talks about strengths, people's strengths, he talks about hardships. It's always a balance with Doug, it's always balanced, you know. It's never all of this or all of this. He does a perfect balance with the two and he always says that the old Mi'kmaw stories, some of the endings were pretty ugly but so is life. Life is beautiful but it's also ugly. You gotta have that balance. That's what I hear when Doug says those opening and closing prayers.

Frank Meuse Remembers

I remember Doug Knockwood and Lawrence Paul coming down and speaking with my parents and other people in the community, talking about their agency and what they could do to help.

I used to hear the stories about when our people weren't allowed to go into drinking establishments, they weren't allowed to buy alcohol from the liquor stores, they weren't even allowed to have alcohol in their possession. People would smuggle different types of homemade liquor into the reserves and sell it to our people and I think of how devastating that was. There are stories of people just mixing up concoctions and I heard some of our relations died from different types of alcohol poisoning. I can't imagine what it must have been like living through that era where alcohol was destroying social and family connections of a community.

Even though some of the laws had changed, we were still dealing with the chaos of alcohol in my parents' generation. We were all still feeling the effects and we found it difficult to live with a loved one who had addictions. We couldn't understand alcoholism and its complexities. Because my mother never drank she could never explain to us children what was going on around us or why. So when these outreach workers came to our community, people like Doug and Lawrence, they could give us some answers. Looking back at my first encounter with Doug, what stands out the most was his soft-spoken gentleness, sincerity and smile which broke down any immediate fears or reluctance. It never felt like he was there just for a job. We knew he was there to help because he wanted to help.

Doug and Lawrence started off just talking to individual family members and then later had small community functions where people could come and share and talk. We had discussions about what alcohol is, why it is in our community and how do we control it instead of it controlling us. However, we were challenged ourselves on how to drink sociably as we were still seeing the misuse of alcohol and peer pressure to always have one more drink.

Doug introduced three programs to our community: AA (directed at the individuals), Al-Anon (for the families who were affected) and Alateen (for the youth to talk about the effects and diversions). Initial conversations Doug had with my mother and others in the community, and the establishment of the NADACA [Native Alcohol and Drug Abuse Counselling Association] programs, allowed us to understand more about alcoholism as a disease and how to cope as a family or community member.

We don't realize the impact individuals have on ourselves believe Doug's and Lawrence's

that we

about how to move together as a community, what we felt would be the main things that would have to be looked at: education, housing and health. And at one point our community considered going "dry."

I remember on a personal note, I woke up one day and asked, "What does it mean to be Mi'kmaq?" I went through this course of elimination, saying, "Well, I don't think me misusing alcohol, drugs or tobacco is it." We were told by our Elders that a little dose of something could be good medicine but to overdo it could be just the opposite. For example, to watch an Elder use small quantities of tobacco in ceremonies was good medicine where on the other hand to watch someone inhale cigarettes on a daily basis is unhealthy. It was really interesting to go through all those transformations as an individual. When I look at our community now, I can tell that there's more options for everyone to make healthier choices, with emphasis put on our younger people. And it's not just alcohol, but other challenges that they're going to have to cope with to find where things fit in their lives and community as we move forward.

When we looked at the people who have inspired us, like Doug Knockwood and others in the community who refrained from alcohol, it showed us that you can have a happy life without it. It's great to have these people still around helping us with the next generation with their stories and encouragement.

As a Mi'kmaw nation we have a lot to be thankful to Doug for what he's been able to accomplish in his life. (I might even let him have a few extra strokes on the golf course when we play.) Even though he's never been in a high profile leadership role, he's done so many little things in great ways that have made him a leader in his own right. His humility keeps him at the grassroots level where I feel he's had the most impact. Doug has never given up, even with all the hardship he's had in his life he's still been able to come out the other end and continue on helping other people.

In my view a respected Elder is someone who has acquired a great amount of humility in their life, which allows them to speak their truth in a peaceful way. Sometimes you can tell a respected Elder by how they can light up a room, and as they make time for each person in the room no matter their background, when people leave many feel that they were that Elder's pet. I agree that Doug Knockwood is a respected Elder in Mi'kma'ki and I'm also honoured to call him a friend.

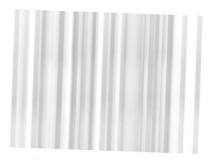

Inspiration in His Community

For a person like Doug, retirement did not mean inactivity. In fact, in the years since he officially retired from his work at the treatment centre, he has been actively attending meetings, conferences and planning sessions, and seeking to further his education. Throughout his life he has had to deal with many tragedies, yet he has been able to draw on his inner strength to move forward in spite of difficulties that would have derailed a lesser person. In his retirement he is called upon to participate in all kinds of events. Today, in his late 80s, he is a highly respected Elder continually providing counselling, a listening post and inspiration to people in his community and beyond.

Going Back to School

I still had a tendency to burden myself with the lack of education. Even though I had those top jobs in the Northwest Territories and Nova Scotia and New Brunswick, in the back of my head it still said, "You know you can't play the game." So I decided to go back to school.

I enrolled in a program that was conducted by Saint Mary's University in the old Normal School building in Truro. The first year I only stayed for about a month and a half. I didn't feel academically inclined and had trouble spelling. When I was working I could write a report because I knew my secretary would correct it for me. But I didn't have a secretary with me when I was in the classroom. But I still wanted to continue with the program.

The next year Kathy said, "Doug, I'll help you as much as I can but I can't go to the classroom with you." And that's how I decided to go back. She did as much as she could for me. I still have difficulty with it. I'll never lose it, the residential school. It was with me my whole life. I just couldn't shake it. I enjoyed the program but after a year I didn't go back.

Errol Sharpe Remembers

In the fall of 1990 I was teaching an extension course called The Political Economy of Atlantic Canada for Saint Mary's University in Truro. Nova Scotia. On the first day of class

Mi'kmaw man who spoke

was captivating. On the night that it was Doug's turn to make his class presentation he asked me before class if he could introduce his presentation in the Mi'kmaw language. I remember saying to him, "It's your presentation Doug. You can do whatever you want." After speaking in his native tongue for three or four minutes, he stopped and asked the class if they understood what he had said. Of course, no one did. This was his way of explaining how he felt when he was forced to speak English, a language he did not know, when he went to the Shubenacadie Indian Residential School.

Doug proceeded to tell the class about his horrendous experience at the school. For most of the students, it was the first time they had heard a personal account of the school. When he finished, there was dead silence. After what seemed like a long time, a student in the front row looked up at Doug with tears running down her cheeks and asked, "Sir, what can we do?" Doug stood silently for a number of seconds, then quietly said, "Come visit me. Come to my home. Come to my community and meet my people." It was an answer that no one, including myself, expected.

Earlier in the year I had noticed that Doug's wife used to pick him up after class. The Indian Brook First Nation, where

Doug lived, was on my way home and only a few minutes off the highway, so I offered to drive him, and he accepted. It gave me an opportunity to talk with Doug each week on the way to his home. Often we would linger in Doug's driveway and chat. On the night of his class presentation, I remarked on his answer to overcome their fear and get to know his people. He explained to me that much of the problem of racism and discrimination is based on fear. He reasoned that if people could just get a chance to meet him in his own home and his people in their community, the sense of fear — fear of the unknown, fear based on years of false information — would be overcome.

Doug and I became friends. I later found out that he was a golfer, and for a number of years we would get together on a few occasions each summer to play golf.

I fondly remember the chats on those evenings driving from Truro to Indian Brook. I admired Doug's patience, his ability to listen. I will never forget a class in which another student was making his presentation. The student talked of his experience of teaching in a First Nation in Northern Manitoba. The student was relaying a story about how the teachers had to barricade themselves in their residence to protect themselves from the "Indians." I was annoyed about the way he was talking about the people and went to intervene. Doug stood up, held up his hand and said, "Mr. Sharpe, let him speak. I want to hear what he has to say." After listening for a period of time, Doug again arose and said, "Okay, you can stop now. That's enough." By the time the student was done speaking, there was an aura of quiet hostility toward him in the room. If Doug hadn't interrupted me when I was about to silence the student, the class would not have had the opportunity to learn the lesson that they did.

When the student sat down, Doug asked him, "Why did you go to Manitoba?" The student said something like, "I needed a job, and I thought I could help these people." The message was not lost of the rest of the class. Then Doug continued by saying, "Do you intend to go back there to teach?" When the student answered yes, Doug quietly asked, "Will you come to my home and have a talk before you return to Manitoba?" Doug's

be here long after

During many of our chats on the road to Indian Brook, Doug spoke of his grandfather and his dream of writing a book about him. I often said to Doug, "You should write your own story." Years later, in the fall of 2014, we got together and began recording interviews — interviews that have become the body of this book. Today, Doug is greatly honoured as a respected Elder of his people. Knowing Doug, becoming a friend of Doug's and listening to his life story and his counsel have been among the highlights of my life. Thank you, Doug, for being my friend. You have often expressed your concern about your lack of education and your trouble with writing. But my friend, listening to you, hearing the story of your life and absorbing your wisdom have been for me and for so many, many others the greatest gift. I am greatly honoured and privileged to be a part of facilitating the telling of your story.

Tragedy Again

Kathy was having these headaches off and on through the last part of our life together. These headaches would come. She'd lie down, five minutes, gone. Then she could carry on the same as anyone else. Then one day she went to Pictou Landing for a business meeting of some kind. When she was driving back she called me twice. She said, "You got the kids packed? Everything's ready to go." I called her and she was at the bottom of Mount Thom. She said, "I got a headache. I'm going to have a little rest." "Where are you?" I asked again. "I'm at the foot of Mount Thom." I waited for probably a good twenty minutes, half an hour and phoned again. "Where are you?" I asked. She said, "I am at the top of Mount Thom. The headache's back, though." I called her again and asked, "Whereabouts are you?" She said, "I am in Truro. I'm having a smoke and I'll pick up the apples." We didn't eat apples. I said to Ben, who worked at the treatment centre, "Drive me to Truro."

On the way to Truro we saw the van that Kathy was driving coming towards us on the other side. It was in the outside lane, foot to the floor. Dust was flying. "Oh my god, Ben, look." Good thing we had a phone. I picked up the phone and called her, "What the hell you going to?" "I'm going after the apples." "Pull over and stop and I'll go with you. Slow down and talk to me. Ease over in the other lane. You in the other lane?" "Yes." "Okay. Ease off, slow down. Pull over on the shoulder so you can stop." "I am." "Are you off the road?" "Yes." She said, "Oh, Doug, my headache." And that's the last words she said. I got Ben to turn around and we came back. When we got there, the van was in the ditch. She was squashed under the steering wheel. There was a man standing there writing. He said, "Everything [the ambulance] is coming. You're the husband?" I don't know who he was. He was a man who was travelling. He said he had a case in Halifax.

I couldn't lift her because she was wedged under the seat. Just then the ambulance came on the other side and the attendant ran across the road with the stretcher and opened the van door and had the stretcher laid out. And we go inside and he said, "Oh, I'm going to have a hard trouble getting her out of there." And I said, "I don't think I can help you." He looked at me, "Oh, my god, Doug." He was our scout leader. Kathy and I were scout guides. He looked up at me. Tears came to his eyes. He picked her up from right under the wheel with her arms laid out. That was an experience I'll never forget. I sat there. I couldn't drive. I called a friend of ours and they came. Told 'em what happened. They drove us home. Kids dropped their books off and things and we loaded up the van and went into Truro 'cause the ambulance took her to Truro and we followed them in. We went ... didn't stand a chance. That's all I need to

Peggy MacNeil Remembers

When I met Doug and Kathy? What I can say? They were just such a compassionate couple. You could just see that the love was there. They were each such positive people. Never negative. And their love for one another was the same. He had had a rocky road in life. But she was his life and he was hers. They were just so compatible that way. When you first met them, you loved them. I first met Kathy in 1983, at the Eskasoni School. She was in the administration and I was a teacher. She was my boss, but she treated me like her peer and I respected that in Kathy. It also never interfered with our friendship. Sure, we might have a disagreement over work at a staff meeting, but with Kathy, work was left at work. When it was over, we just got back in the car and laughed it off and we never discussed our work outside of the workplace. I believe this made both of our jobs much easier.

She was honest, sincere and loyal not only to her family, but also to her job. To a good teacher, children are number one. And that's what education should be: For the kids, not anyone else.

How devoted was Doug to Kathy? I can remember him getting up at five or six in the morning, just so he could drive into Sydney to get her some coffee. And there they'd be, out in a canoe on the lake at sunrise, enjoying every moment.

They loved their kids. Their kids were everything to them.

She wasn't worried whether everything was shining in the house. For her, it was Doug and the kids first. She used to say that there would be a day when everyone was gone, and then the house would be shiny and clean. And now I see myself today with my apartment all tidy with nobody to mess it all up, and now I've come to miss just having someone around to make a mess!

When we met I was a new mother too, so we hit it off over that. Our priority on the weekend was the kids. Everybody else waited. Whatever we were going to do, we planned something with all of our kids involved. We made a happy life and a friendship out of that, and spent many weekends camping together.

Once we got the kids tucked in, Doug would often go off to a meeting in Eskasoni or somewhere. Kathy and I would sit out at night, under the stars, and just talk. We'd share what was happening in our lives, our ups and downs. She quickly became the type of friend that I knew I could depend on for life. One of the best things that ever happened to me in my life was Kathy's friendship.

My father had started to get ill when I met Kathy, and she was a strength for me. I was very close to my dad. With cancer, it's very traumatic for a family to go through that loss for the first time and it really hits home. Kathy worried about Doug and his health, but she was never negative about it and didn't want any pity. I think that her influence taught me how to handle sickness in my own family. I lost my own husband and my dad, and Kathy was always there for me.

I remember Doug calling me from Halifax, telling me Kathy was dying. I felt like I lost a piece of my heart. I was the last one to leave the hospital. I couldn't leave her, I just kept thinking, "C'mon girl, you're gonna wake up. Fight this!" Eventually I went back home and then went to Doug's for the wake and funeral. It was a difficult one. I remember getting in the car after her funeral. I cried all the way home to Sydney.

I can't wait till the day I see her again, but I know she's watching over me. We used to say, "You keep an eye on my children and I'll keep an eye on yours." She's doing a darned

just sweating from dancing and she was ~~~ her. So I was talking to her and I forget how it went but anyways she said, "You're coming back in I'll have to have a dance with you." She said, "My group is leaving." And I said, "Okay, we're on for the next." It was a year later I met her again and we had a dance. And that's how our relationship started. I met her at the dance in Cambridge. That's when we made our date. We went out in the afternoon and I invited her out to supper and I took her to the Five Fishermen restaurant in Halifax. We had a nice dinner and I drove her home and I said, "I'll see you later." "Okay." I started to visit her. After a while it became a habit. We were married in December 2007.

Michelle Remembers

I was at a dance. I lived in the Valley, and I had come to a roundup in Truro with a bunch of ladies. I was a smoker back then and I went outside to have a smoke. When I was standing outside, I saw Doug there, catching his breath. At the time I didn't know he had one lung. We had a conversation, and he made me feel like a million bucks. He was just charming. I was ready to leave, but before I went home he said, "You owe me a dance." I didn't see him for a year.

A year after that I met him in Three Mile Plain, at another roundup. This time he asked me for a dance. And so we danced all night. At the end of the evening, we started chatting. He asked me if I played golf. I said no. He told me that if I wanted to come with him, he'd show me how to play.

He came to get me for a round of golf two weeks after. I had just left an abusive relationship and I was living with my teenage son, so I didn't bring men into my apartment. He came to meet me in Wolfville at a coffee shop. I didn't realize then that he's always late, so when he didn't show up, I just left. I went walking and didn't make it back to my place until after lunchtime. There was a voicemail message from him, saying that we must have missed each other and to give him a call. He didn't leave a phone number though.

In September, he called me to go for a nice meal at the Five Fishermen and to go dancing at the Legion. I had no clue what the Five Fishermen was. I told my daughter, and she just said, "If he's going to bring you there, you'd better keep him."

After that, I saw him once a month, then every few weeks. After knowing him for over a year, he asked if I would like to come and visit his place. I started to live there, and by the following fall I had moved there officially.

We took a trip to Prince Edward Island, and that's where I guess I challenged him with the question, "Should we be a couple?" We had to talk about the topic. So I asked him, "Is your heart big enough to love two people?" Because he had loved Kathy, and he still loved her memory. He told me, "Yes."

After we had lived together for a while, we took a trip to California by train. Doug told me that he had always wanted to visit the San Francisco trolleys. I was a teacher for the deaf, with my summers off, so that next summer we went. It was five days on the train from Montreal to San Francisco. We stayed for a week and it was very nice. When we got home, in the fall, I went back to school.

One night, Doug just said, "If we can travel together, maybe

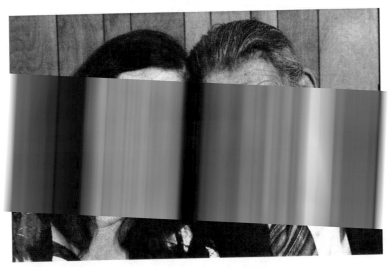

Doug and Michelle

we should get married." I was like, "Really?" He always said that I had this part planned. But that's not true. I had a friend who was a justice of the peace in Pugwash, and by December we were married.

Now, when I met Doug, I was twenty-some years in teaching and I had to make a choice. I couldn't keep working full time and be married to him. To enjoy our life while he was healthy and to have our time together — because of our difference in age — I made the choice to take early retirement.

Being married to Doug has been a bit difficult, but not because of him. On the reserve, I was an outsider, and it's taken a little while to fit in. To many people I'm still just "Doug's wife." I don't think I even have a name. Kathy was very involved in the community and she had a position within the community.

The other thing — many of the twelve-step members were really protective of Doug. They were concerned I would take advantage of him. And there were a lot of women that were very fond of him. There were a lot of worried people, asking, "How long have you known each other? How did you meet?" By the end I just started messing with them. I'd say, "We just met! I've known him for twenty-four hours." It's also been a question of living with an extended family. It's taken time to make things work. I'm also coming from a family where alcohol was present. And at the time I met Doug, my life was a shambles too. But it's been good for Doug and I to be together. Because I'm a "program person," it really is nice to live in a house with someone who has found sobriety. Living the twelve steps makes life so much easier, even for a couple. If I couldn't have the program, I couldn't live with him. "That's right," says Doug.

COUNSELLOR AND
HONOURED ELDER

A Natural Teacher

Doug is inherently a teacher. Like all good teachers his great strength is his patience. He leads by example. By living his own life he shows others how to live theirs. He is a leader. Because he is a respected Elder, people still come to him for counselling and direction. In this final section Doug explains how he works.

Being Educated

I worked so much in volunteering in Boston. I went to the prisons and rehab centres all the time. And I didn't realize that I was getting knowledge from all these guys that I talked to. And when I came back to Nova Scotia, I was able to utilize all this and go to different reserves and put the program in. And they started to call me to do extra work on the different places, like Parrsboro, Halifax, Truro, Sydney and of course Indian Brook And I was always working with a cross-section of Aboriginal people and non-Aboriginal. The non-Aboriginal people even hired me to do the workshop because they wanted to learn about how to work with our Mi'kmaw people. So they would hire me to do these sessions. And so as a result of this, I was called to many places, and I said I'll get an education for myself and that's when I put in to go to George Brown College. Lawrence and I agreed that I could go. He said, "Doug, you got everything rolling so well even I can handle it." I said I'd like to go and he said sure. I got the first year in and was in the second year, but they opened the Native college in the old Bomarc missile site. And my son was on the board of directors.

Don Fitzpatrick Remembers

Doug is what we call "old fashioned." He still travels everywhere and that's because of the way he grew up in the program. Because for a long time, there were only two, then five, then seven groups around Nova Scotia. And travelling around was how you got other groups started. Guys from one group would put on meetings in another town and they would load up as many car-fulls as they could get. They'd travel from Shubie to ... Sydney. They'd go from Truro to Baddeck. And

Doug heard what was happening ...
streets have that strong fellowship, and my uncle and Doug sure had that bond.

They had refused to take my uncle at the detox at the Nova Scotia Hospital. They had pretty much said that he was hopeless, that he had been there ten or twelve times and that they couldn't do anything more for him. The last time he was in the hospital, he went into the DTs.

It was Doug who was able to get him back into the hospital. He was there for him for the thirty-day detox, along with another twelve-step member. They looked after his spiritual needs. At the end of those thirty days, they took him home and cleaned him up. And he never had to drink again.

Subsequently, my uncle and Doug both sponsored me and taught me how to live one day at a time without alcohol. He saved my uncle's life and in turn he saved my life when he became my sponsor. My last drink was May 31, 1989.

This program teaches to give back what was so freely given. It requires that we don't rest on our laurels. If we see another suffering alcoholic, we can't tell them what to do. You're never going to talk someone into getting sober. But we love them and support them. Doug taught me that if you live as a role model, other people will gravitate towards that. And that's the great thing about Doug. Even though I respect him so much for his knowledge and wisdom as an Elder and as a long-time recovered alcoholic, he never told me how to live my life. He just lived his and let me watch.

Those opportunities to support others have come up for me as well. I had a granddaughter who called me up. She said she thought she had a problem with alcohol. She had tried to jump out of a car while it was traveling at sixty miles per hour. When I got to Ontario, I got her to some meetings. I got her mom to go for support. That is what Doug taught me, to give back to some poor other alcoholic.

Doug knows everyone at every meeting, probably in all the Maritimes. In the Native communities, in the non-Native communities, wherever he goes. You just could never estimate the impact that he's had on so many families. To bring people back and have them be productive members of society. I know I'm thankful for him for saving my life and the lives of countless others. That's my friend Doug.

AA Philosophy

The AA philosophy is you can't broadcast, you can't go out and say, "Join AA." In AA you have to be very quiet about it and bring a person out to talk to you or you go and talk to them on a private one-to-one basis. And once you've established some communication lines and opened up and talked to that man or woman, then you have a foothold, then you start working towards — you start off with the soft part version and build up to whatever they're on. They're on alcohol, okay. They're on drugs, you have to have somebody else to do that. A lot of us that were alcoholics, we understood the alcoholic procedures, but if you're on drugs we didn't know that. So we had to take guys that understood that. Sort of similar to a hands-on situation. You take a guy or the gal, detox and put 'em in a program. Stay with 'em until whatever time you feel they're strong enough to go on their own. They'd come with you for maybe a month, six weeks, and pretty soon they don't need you.

The program in Sydney was an individual and a group program. There they could go into meetings in the city or in town.

a foothold in understanding ....,

from. It means I can go in there and help them, not to alleviate their hurt and their frustration, but to give them a pathway — a pathway of sobriety so that they can look at their life in a clear-thinking way. I kept them sober long enough that I could work with them after two weeks and sit down and say, "Do you want to go back into this place or that place or do you want to go back to the reserve, the community? Do you want to stay here for a week, ten days or whatever?" I was able to manipulate the circumstances as they were, in order to benefit the person that we could help. I used all the tools that were available in order to help that person. It didn't make any difference who it was. If she wanted to get sober and help herself stay away from it, then this is what we were supposed to do.

You have to work closely with those people. You put them in treatment, if they're willing to go into treatment. You take them and put 'em in treatment. You can't work with anybody who is on alcohol. You got to get them dried out. Five to seven days or whatever. Once you get them over that area where they're not going to have to beg and plead and stuff, then you're able to step in and help them start to clear this up, sitting there with them. And once they've established that you're okay, that you're not there to hurt them, that you're there to help them, the trail becomes a little easier. They have to get some sobriety under their belt, and they're thinking away from alcohol and drugs. It's very difficult to stop drinking if you've been at it for a long time. Once you're able to establish this rapport with them to keep them away from that place, that mud hole, then you start to move them in the right direction. Once you get them in this right direction, then you sort of have the hand, you get a hold of the hand and you're helping them up over this muddy road. Once they see that you are there to help them get over this muddy road, the road becomes much easier for them to walk. You lead them and you give them the program to go by. Five days, five days is your chance to get dried out and to think things over and say, "I got a chance." So you stay with that person and help them to establish some guidelines for himself or herself. And once they're able to do this, I used to find that the guys and the gals who are counsellors are able to take over and they lead them onto the good side of the road. And this is what a lot of them needed, was that support, that wisdom, because everybody said, "Oh, you're a fucking drunk. Keep the fuck out of my sight."

They have to build their strength from within. Because for so long they look at you and think, "you fucking drunk." Or somebody gives you in an argument and is waiting for you to stand up and defend yourself. And when you're on skid row and a drunk there's no way you can defend yourself. Everybody takes a shot at you and away you go, arse over kettle somewhere. But you get help because it says for you to get up and defend yourself. If you don't defend yourself, nobody else will. So this is when you start to run wild. When you get in there and you know in your mind they're not going to make you go further down than I am.

It didn't make any difference what nationality. If they were alcoholics, they're alcoholics. And the only thing you could do is give them that drink to level them off and hope that they'll come with you to a meeting of people that understand and help you. Or you go to one of the established programs, AA, Alateen or whatever. But you have to build that person up strong enough so that they'll go to these places.

And they depend on you even when they go in those doors. They're still there, looking for your help.

I can work with the guy in Indian Brook and the guy in Halifax at the same time because they're both suffering from the same disease

come and sit with me on the chair.

Come on. Let's go. Come on back." And I'd say no. He spent hours with me trying to get me to come back to the reserve. That's before his father kicked me out of the house. And it was guys like this that tried to help you, but John didn't have the right tools to work with to bring me back. Because John just wanted the best for me and the only way he knew how to do that was to bring me back here where he thought I would be protected, a place to stay, a place to eat, things like this.

But that's not all, it's only part of the recovery. But to get well, you have to cut the line here and say I can't touch that without — I can't talk to them people. It's a hell of a thing when your friend in the morning comes up and shows you a quart of wine and says, "Hey, it's on me." And you get sober and, "No I don't want it." And a lot of times that's why you take it. That person goes to work or wherever he was going. He gave you that even though in his heart he felt he was helping you, but he didn't know he was making it worse for you. So somehow I gotta get around and tell him, "I'm sorry, but I can't drink this." And then I go around the bush again and say the reason why I can't. And in the end he will appreciate what I have told him because he doesn't know anything about this himself. And he'd say, "Oh, shit, I didn't know that, Doug. One drink? One mouthful?" "Yep. Only one mouthful and I'm gone." And he couldn't believe that.

There are two parts to being an alcoholic, physical and mental. You become dependent on the drug, and one drink can trigger it all over again. There is also the part where you have to overcome the reason why you became an alcoholic. That's how you work on yourself. They gave me all the tools to work with. The tools are to stay away from people that drink, stay as clean as I possibly can, don't take that first drink. That was the most important thing. You don't touch that first drink, you won't have to worry about taking another one. Today. And also exist today for me. You know there's no guarantee I'll be sober tomorrow. God, I hope I am. But those are the things I have to watch for. And it was a long time before I realized that. These counsellors used to talk to me about, you know, "Doug, it's one drink that's throwing you off the wagon." "Oh no, I can handle one drink." See, I didn't understand that one drink.

Bill Partridge Remembers

When I started working in the field of addictions and mental health, I became interested in First Nations issues. Working in the field of addictions, I knew that I would need guidance. Clinical supervision. I needed someone to teach me the ways and wake me up to what I already knew. Doug woke me up to what I was, a healer. He taught me one of the most powerful teaching techniques, which was "modelling of behaviour." He reinforced my own sobriety in me by displaying how to live life as I was supposed to be, a happy, sober, man. The way Creator wanted me to be.

In my work as an addictions therapist, I ended up going to Davis Inlet. In 1990, Health and Welfare Canada, Medical Services Branch, sent me there on a month-long contract to do a community assessment. When I got there, it was clear to me that this was a community in crisis. They had the highest rate of suicide of anywhere in the world. When the contract with Health and Welfare ran out, I decided that I would commit to stay and help the healing process however I could, and stay as long as I was needed. I was hired in the capacity of an addictions therapist by the Mushuau Innu Band Council, and I wound up staying for four years.

At the time, they weren't getting any help from the

of bureaucrats. Some of these was all overwhelming for the community.

I knew, after working with the Elders, that there was a need to slow things down. These Elders were only in their fifties and sixties; life expectancy is low. They were young people who were needed to make big decisions for the community — and they needed some reassurance. We needed to bring in some heavyweight healers to help them survive this. So we brought in Ovide Mercredi, who at the time was the National Chief of the Assembly of First Nations, along with Maggie Hodgson from Poundmaker's Lodge and the Nechi Institute, and Doug Knockwood.

When Doug came, I remember crying in his arms. I was in crisis. At that point, to have a friend who was so sober and strong, that I could trust — it was a wonderful feeling. I brought Doug in specifically to work with the Elders in the community. To support them, to reinforce their culture, to share his experiences, and his strength and his hope. I felt he could help teach them how to cope with what they were dealing with, how to learn from it, work through it and come out the other side. Doug has these intrinsic skills: how to touch a person's soul with respect; how to love unconditionally again; how to love people back to sanity and how to do it with humour, to a point where they laugh like children, even amidst a crisis. These aren't acquired skills. As a healer, you're given these gifts to use as a modality in the healing process.

Doug travelled with me in the country, across the frozen sea and barrens. We would travel in minus 40 degree weather, for days on end, eating caribou, geese and fish. The nuns were afraid we might get cold, so they gave us these mustard yellow coats. I had one and Doug had the other. It was a funny time to see us in these coats, even amidst all that tragedy. A couple of years later I brought him back to the community again. This time, there was some cause for celebration. I also had him do several workshops for the Elders. He spoke with them on how to operate in the European world and yet still keep their dignity. As an educator and a teacher, he's taught me the ways of the Mi'kmaq, and for that I'll always love him and respect his spirit in this life and the next. He's a powerful man. And even a better friend.

A Gentle Approach

When talking with people, I try to keep my voice low constantly, all the time because they're so used to people coming in — and a lot of our guys or gals that are working in the field, their attitude is not very good, because a lot of them feel that they got the job, they don't need to do this, they don't need to do that. They figured they were more important. They forget about who's putting the money on the table. So they just run roughshod over the people there. I never had to do that, even with my own people. I had to manhandle a few of them but it was because of a lack of understanding. Probably didn't want to go to a meeting but they were required to go because of the court system.

The crux of the program is to build from your contact. You start out by introducing yourself. The guys or the girls don't know you. So you talk to them about different things in life and you start off very slowly. Maybe you just go for a coffee and you give them some information or knowledge of what you're doing or what you're there for. And you stay with that as long as you can before they throw you out the door. Communication is important. They'll start out with you and they'll agree with you but as soon as they get that first drink, you're a son of a bitch! Just like that, turns over. And then of course

you have to deal with

It just goes in here and out there. But once you start to sober up, it has a different meaning. You hear people say "bad as that Indian." It's stereotyping. Constantly. All the time. Gotta turn this hearing aid off, and this one up good and loud. Like when I first started out I had a hard time to stay sober. Four years? I was a fighter. If you didn't say the right thing, then you had to go 'cause there'd be flying chairs or something. I wasn't proud of that but it was the only thing I knew to protect myself.

The talking stick helped me to be a listener but also to be aggressive when the time needed to be. If I listen to you during a session and if you were going around in a circle, I would listen to what's going on and if you said something that I didn't agree with, then I would listen and I would listed to the other people. I usually sat in the middle. I'd find wherever the instructor is. I want to be facing him so I could watch your eyes and your expression. I learned how to read the expression. My mother, God rest her soul, was a great one. You know, she would look at somebody for five minutes and tell whether that person was a good person or a bad person. And she said, "All you have to do is this." And she told me the things I had to watch for that tells me about the person, their vocabulary and their physical appearance. And she never had an English education, it was all Mi'kmaw.

Trying to fight fire with fire is a poor way to go about it because there's no end to that fire. Either I'm throwing a log on it or you're throwing a log on it. Because the fire is lowering down and we have to build it up. So I throw my five cents' worth on and when it starts to wear down, it's time for you to throw your five cents on. So we're able to argue or do whatever we're doing. As long as we keep them sparks flying out of that fire, we're going to be okay. But when sparks stop flying out of that fire, then we gotta watch out because somebody gonna get hurt. Somewhere along the way, somebody has to intervene to help overcome those situations. You hear them all the time whether you're drunk or sober. You hear them on the street now. I hear them all the time. It doesn't bother me. Today, it doesn't bother me.

Respected and Honoured Elder

In his later years Doug has received many accolades. Officially he was retired but he has remained very active. In 2004 he received the Grand Chief Donald Marshall Sr. Elder Achievement Award at Government House in Halifax. The award was in recognition of his tireless work. In the years since he received the award, he has continued to be

Doug receiving the Grand Chief Donald Marshall Sr. Elder Achievement Award, 2003

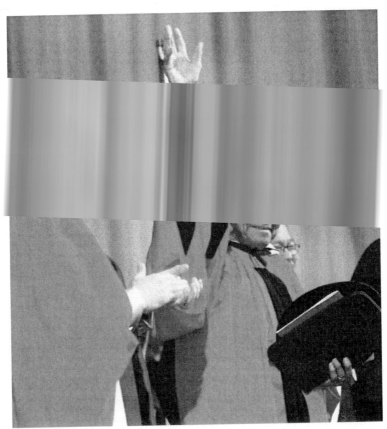

Doug receiving an honorary doctorate of humanities from Acadia University (photo: Dan Callis)

called upon to offer prayers at events all over the Maritime region and abroad. He is an invited lecturer and honoured guest at university classrooms and at innumerable conferences across Nova Scotia.

Doug is regularly called upon to offer a blessing. He offered the Aboriginal blessing during the 2014 visit of the Prince of Wales to Canada, as he did when Queen Elizabeth visited in 2010. People are both comforted and inspired by his words. Doug's prayers are always spontaneous and adapted to the situation. Once asked if he had a prayer written down, he replied, "It is written in my head."

Over the years Doug has continued to sit on many boards. He sits on the Elder Advisory Council of the Mi'kmawey Debert Cultural Centre. The centre was established by the Confederacy of Mainland Mi'kmaq and is dedicated to sharing, protecting and exploring the stories and lives of our earliest ancestors and those who have come after them in Mi'kma'ki. He serves on the board of the Public Service Alliance of Canada and the Aboriginal Health Research Program. He works with the Sipekne'katik (Indian Brook) School Board, coordinating "talking circles" for teachers, staff and parents. He is a past board member of the Treatment Directors of Canada and the Rehabilitation Counselors of Alberta.

In May 2015 he received an honorary doctorate of humanities from Acadia University. In his concluding remarks at the convocation, he said, "Now at 85 years old I would like to share with you a list of qualities that I believe will help you in your career and personal life. They helped me through my journey.

1. Be determined — do not give up.
2. Ask for help when you need it.
3. Keep learning to better yourself.
4. Communication skills will open many doors.
5. Do not keep grudges, and let go of your anger.
6. Enjoy your life in the moment.
7. Listen for your brother or sister who may need help.
8. And specifically do not forget to be yourself."

Debbie Toney Remembers

I met Doug in 2014, in Millbrook. I heard him speak about his experiences in residential school. I was so overwhelmed by his stories, his passion and his beliefs. What he said was dear to my heart. I'm First Nations and have many family members that also went to the residential school. But I had never heard a lot of the stories until I heard Doug's. At first it broke my heart.

I met him later that summer at the Mawiomi we had over

Doug after receiving the Order of Nova Scotia (photo: Stephen Brake)

four days at Acadia. Elders, community members — Indigenous people from everywhere — came down to Acadia, and we kept a sacred fire. Doug and I had many conversations and he taught me a lot. He shared stories on the ways of the land. He talked about old people's stories and how stories were passed on. All kinds of things went on. At the end of the Mawiomi, Doug presented me with the talking stick that he was given when he was going through alcoholism.

I came back to Acadia to study with one of my professors, Cynthia Alexander. Together we discussed a few times about getting Doug an honorary doctorate. I had never done anything like this before, and there was a lot of paperwork to get through.

Cynthia helped me through it. Together, we presented the suggestion to Acadia, and they said yes.

I felt he was a good candidate because of everything he had gone through and the teachings he had brought out the other side — the entire aspect of his life, his traditions and his teachings. He's a very respected Elder. There are lots out there that are deserving, don't get me wrong. But to me, I couldn't think of anyone more deserving than Doug.

The headline in the October 12, 2016, issue of the *Ku'Ku'Kwes News* read: "Mi'kmaq Elder Doug Knockwood Receives Order of Nova Scotia." On receiving the award, Doug said, "I never thought that I would ever accomplish, you know, the things that I've accomplished. And this, I guess, is the top of the cake. Each and every one of the people in my community that I had a close association with had to do with where I am today. Because if it wasn't for them, I wouldn't have been able to build my life's roadmap."

Glen Remembers

My dad is one of the most amazing people I have ever met. He has taught me so much about all aspects of life. As far back as I can remember, he's been an example of what it means to be *l'nu*.

When I was a child living in Sydney he was the only Native person I knew and in many ways he became the example of what it meant to me to be Mi'kmaq. The first memories I have of my father are ones where he is very stern and grumpy. I joke and say that my earliest memories are of him saying, "No," because whenever I would ask my mother for something she would never say no she would only say, "Ask your father." I would never end up asking him because I learned from experience what his answer would be.

My father stopped being "no" for me when I was 13, and my mother passed from a brain aneurysm. For a while the remaining members of my immediate family were in mourning just trying to figure out how our lives were to move forward. My father really stepped up and became both our father and mother. He both guided and protected as well as being nurturing and

has been so much vast

it appear as if the only way we can have access to that time period was through these history books. However, the moment she said that the Great Depression began in 1929, bells and whistles started to go off in my head. I remembered that my father was born in 1929 and to me that was very exciting, because here I am sitting in a class of my peers everyone learning about the past through secondhand knowledge and at home I had a person who lived during and through those times and is still alive today.

I resolved at that moment to be more than just my father's son. I was going to be my father's friend. When my dad picked me up from school that day he took me to Tim Horton's, bought me a peach juice, that old fountain peach juice they used to have, and I started to ask him questions about his life. This began my obsession with my father because I began to see him as this living vessel of great experience, which I could now draw upon. I learned what it was like to be around when things like penicillin, transistor radios, helicopters, electric razors, jet engines, nuclear reactors, bikinis, frisbees, velcro, microwave ovens, credit cards, holograms and satellites were first starting to become widespread. My own father, who began his life living off the land in a small self-sustained Mi'kmaw community in Newville Lake, had personally experienced so much change in the world and somehow he was still really *cool*! He didn't let his hardships age him or make him become hardened in his ways. For years I would ask him about his life and learn the stories of his youth and of his growing up to become a man, about his time in residential school, the mistakes he has made and how he has learned from them. He taught me about the power of the mind, and our connection to the world around us and to each other.

My dad is a great speaker and an even better storyteller. As far back as I can remember my dad has always been giving public talks, workshops and seminars. There were many times in my life where I would meet people who, upon finding out my father was Doug Knockwood, would go on at great length about how my father has saved them or helped them or said the right thing at the right time in a down point in their lives. When I would go back to Dad and tell him I met so-and-so and they said, "Hi and thank you for changing their life," he would always remind me that you cannot change people. People can only change themselves. It seemed paradoxical that these people were sure that Dad did something to change their lives for the better and my dad being sure that they did it themselves.

As I grew up listening to the many stories Dad would tell, one thing became very clear. When Dad tells stories, he tells them in a way that captures you and plops you right in the middle of the event as if you were re-living it yourself. I attribute this skill to our culture, where storytelling is one the primary ways in which we communicate valid and useful experiences from one generation to the next. I have listened and re-lived some of my dad's mistakes just by hearing him tell the story. In this way I can learn the lessons he learned without having to actually go through the stressful experience myself. He taught me that storytelling is actually what us humans are doing all the time. We tell stories. Dad would say there is power in stories, they can help you or harm you depending on how you tell it. In that I learned one of the many way in which my dad "changes" ~~ "helps" people. He tells them a story in which they can play . ...defines their whole experience.

Decem...

upon to offer his wisdom and his praye...

cial events. For example, during the week of November 12–16, 2017, he attended the second Mi'kmaw Child and Welfare Symposium in Dartmouth. On December 5, he was honoured at an Elders dinner at the Mi'kmaw Friendship Centre in Halifax. And he celebrated his 88th birthday a week early because, during the week of December 10–16, he attended a hockey tournament in Truro, Nova Scotia. In February 2018 Doug celebrated fifty-four years of sobriety.

CHRONOLOGY

Birth	December 11, 1929
Parents	Freeman Bernard Knockwood and Ann Mary Knockwood

1935	RCMP take Doug to residential school
1936	Doug's father won court battle releasing Doug and his brother from residential school
1936–40	attended Halfway River West School
1940–41	worked for Gordon Pettigrew on farm
1942–43	worked for farmers
1944–48	worked as labourer around Springhill Junction
1948	joined reserve army, North Nova First Highland Battalion
1950	joined Canadian Special Forces 25th Brigade
1951	joined army's 27th Brigade in Aldershot, Nova Scotia
1952	sent to Valcartier, Quebec, for training for Germany
1952	took a boat from Quebec City to Holland, and by train to Hanover, Germany
1953	returned to Canada, stationed at Aldershot
1954	sent to Gagetown, NB, diagnosed with tuberculosis. December 14, 1954, discharged from army
1955–1959	treated for TB in Shelburne Hospital and Kentville Sanatorium, removed one lung and five ribs
1959–60	treated with INH, became a TB survivor
1960–64	from the hospital to skid row

1964	went to Boston
1070	co-founder of Alcohol and Drug Treatment Program for Mi'kmaw people in Nova Scotia
1972	attended George Brown College, Toronto
-	founder and Executive Director of Arctic House, Yellowknife
1989	returned to Nova Scotia
-	Director Mi'kmaw Healing Lodge, Eskasoni
-	Consultant and Staff Training Coordinator, Native Alcohol and Drug Counselling Association of NS
2000–01	Live-in Treatment Counsellor, Mi'kmaw Friendship Centre, Halifax
	Life Skills Trainer, Springhill Institute, Springhill
2003	received Grand Chief Donald Marshall Sr. Elder Achievement Award
2015	received honorary doctorate of humanities, Acadia University
2016	received Order of Nova Scotia